Dharmishtha V. Oza

Communication Skills in English :

A Beginner's Handbook

CANADIAN
Academic Publishing

2007

Dharmishtha V. Oza

Communication Skills in English :

A Beginner's Handbook

CANADIAN
Academic Publishing

2007

Price : $27.86

First Edition : December, 2007

ISBN : 978-1-926488-78-3

ISBN Allotment Agency : Library and Archives Canada (Govt. of Canada)

Published & Printed by
Canadian Academic Publishing
81, Woodlot Crescent,
Etobicoke,
Toronto, Ontario, Canada.
Postal Code- M9W 6T3
Phone- +1 (647) 633 9712
http://www.canadapublish.com

PREFACE

Communication is the self portrait of an individual presented through words. It is a vital activity of human being. Only human beings are endowed with the ability to use language for expressing their own ideas, feeling, attitudes , opinions , facts etc. And thereby, being supreme to other animals on the earth. It is said that, "Words are the cloths of thoughts, so one should never present words in clumsy manner". We sit in school and listen to teachers. We read books and magazines. We talk to friends, watch television, and communicate over the Internet. The workplace is no different. Experts tell us that70–80 percent of our working time is spent in some kind of communication. We are reading and writing memos, listening to our coworkers, or having one-to-one conversations with our supervisors.

This Book is a roadmap for basics of Communication Skills. The major thrust areas are: Concept of Communication, Methods of Communication, Types and Levels of Communication, Group Discussion, Interviews, Presentation Strategies, Reading Strategies, Listening Skills, Business Letter Writing, Report Writing, Application Writing. Overall objective of this book is to help the reader get an overview of communication skills in nutshell form.

I am grateful to my family members , teachers and friends, for their constant encouragement and help.

Wish You a Joyful Reading !

INDEX

SR. NO.	TOPIC	PAGE NO.
1.	THE CONCEPT OF COMMUNICATION	1
2.	PROCESS OF COMMUNICATION	3
3.	TYPES OF COMMUNICATION	6
4.	LEVELS OF COMMUNICATION	9
5.	OBJECTIVES OF COMMUNICATION	11
6.	GENERAL COMMUNICATION AND TECHNICAL COMMUNICATION	14
7.	LANGUAGE AS A TOOL OF COMMUNICATION	16
8.	BARRIERS TO EFFECTIVE COMMUNICATION	18
9.	TYPES OF VERBAL COMMUNICATION	24
10.	NON-VERBAL COMMUNICATION	26
11.	COMMUNICATION ACROSS CULTURE	30
12.	CONCEPT OF LISTENING	32
13.	TYPES OF LISTENING	33
14.	ACTIVE LISTENING AND PASSIVE LISTENING	36
15.	EMPATHETIC LISTENING	38
16.	TIPS FOR EFFECTIVE LISTENING	40

INDEX

SR. No.	TOPIC	PAGE NO.
17.	BARRIERS TO EFFECTIVE LISTENING	44
18.	PURPOSE OF READING	46
19.	SKIMMING AND SCANNING TECHNIQUE OF READING	48
20.	TIPS TO IMPROVE COMPREHENSION SKILLS	50
21.	PARAGRAPH DEVELOPMENT	53
22.	EFFECTIVE PRESENTATION STRATEGIES	56
23.	GROUP DISCUSSIONS	62
24.	INTERVIEWS	66
25.	BUSINESS LETTER	74
26.	REPORT WRITING	83
27.	PROPOSAL WRITING	91
28.	JOB APPLICATION	94

1. THE CONCEPT OF COMMUNICATION

There is an ancient story which clearly indicates the importance of Communication:

"Emperor Frederick - the 13ᵗʰ century ruler of the Holy Roman Empire – had ordered an experiment in which a group of infants were to be kept in isolated place from hearing human speech from the moment of birth until they spoke their language. The babies were to be raised by nurses who were strictly charged to maintain complete silence when with the babies. The result ? Every one of the babies died. Moral of the Story : You cannot leave without communication.

Human beings and Communication are two interconnected word. You cannot separate communication from human life. Communication is the very basic requirement of any organization and any individual. The English word 'communication' is derived from the Latin noun 'Communis' and the Latin verb 'Communicare' that means 'to make common. to transmit, to impart.' It stands for a natural activity of all human beings to convey opinions, information, ideas, and feelings, emotions to others by words spoken or written, by body language or signs.

Communication has been defined by many theorists; some of these definitions are quoted here :

- According to W.H.Newman, "Communication is an exchange of facts, ideas, opinions or emotions by two or more persons."

- George Vardman in his book `Effective communication of ideas' defines effective commnication as "Purposive interchange, resulting in workable understanding and agreement between the sender and the receiver of the message".

1

- Peter Little says "Communication is the process by which informations are transmitted between individuals or organizations so that an understanding response results.

- Allen Louis says "Communication is the sum of all the things one person does when he wants to create an understanding in the mind of another it involves a systematic and continuous process.

- To quote Norman B. Sigband, "Communication is the transmission and reception of ideas, feelings and attitudes both verbally and non-verbally eliciting a response. It is a dynamic concept underlying all kinds of living systems.

- Dalton McFarland says, "Communication may be broadly defined as the process of meaningful interaction among human beings. More specifically, it is the process by which meanings are perceived and understandings are reached among human beings."

2. PROCESS OF COMMUNICATION

The progression of transmission and interchange of ideas, facts, feelings or actions is known as "Process of Communication". Process of Communication is a full cycle of events from sender to the receiver and back to the sender. Communication is a two way process in which the exchange of ideas links the sender and the receiver towards a mutually accepted direction. The transmission of the sender's ideas to the receiver and the receiver's feedback or reaction to the sender constitutes the communication process. The process of communication may be represented by the following figure showing the steps in the process.

The Communications Process

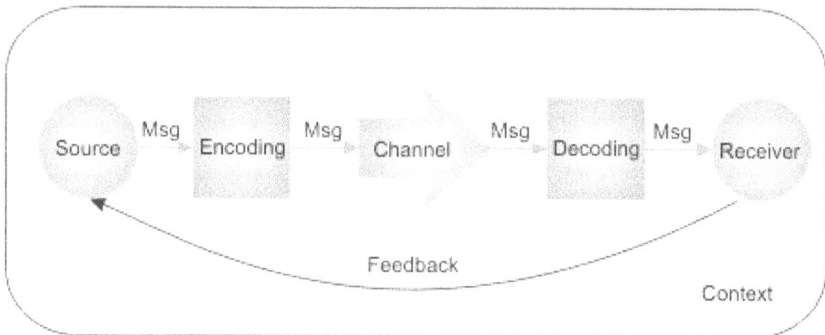

A Process can be understood by this easy example. A boy wants to date a girl. He wants to ask a girl through SMS. First of all, he has some kind of idea about what to type in SMS. So, Formation of Idea in the mind of Sender is first step of Communication. Then he types SMS in his mobile device. This process is called "Encoding" in which you convert your idea into the message. Now, he must need network (mobile card) to send this message to that girl. This network is called "Medium" or "Channel". The person who gets or receives message is a "Receiver", also known as Rx. Here, in our case, Receiver is a girl. When girl receives a message, she reads that message. In more proper words, she understands the message what that boy wants to say. This procedure is known as "Decoding". After decoding, a girl will reply "Yes" or "No" through SMS. This reply is known as "Feedback".

3

Suppose, she slaps him next day. It will Non-verbal feedback , suggesting "No". If she doesn't responds, it means that communication process is one way process.

Easy and Simple ! Now let's learn it by reading in proper language.

- **Sender** : The process of communication starts with a sender, the person who has an idea and wants to convey it to the receiver. In other words, we can say that the person with ideas to share is called sender. So communication process begins with the sender. The Sender is known as Tx.

- **Encoding**: The conversion of the idea in to message by verbal or nonverbal method is called encoding. While encoding a message, one needs to consider what will be interpretation of the message. This process of converting the thought of the sender into message is encoding.

- **Message**: It is an important part of communication. Message is the content that sender wants to convey. A message could be verbal or non-verbal. The thought, idea, emotion or anything that the sender wants to convey is called message.

- **Channel** : The way or the medium of sending the message is called channel. The choice of the medium is influenced by the inter relationship between sender and receiver. It also depends upon the urgency of the message. Medium or channel can be oral, written or it can be non-verbal.

- **Receiver**: The receiver is the person who notices or attaches meaning to the conveyed message. In the best way, if it reaches to the receiver then there is no problem to the receiver to understand the massage properly. In other words, we can say that the receiver is the other party who receives the message of the sender. The Receiver is known as Rx

- **Decoding** : It is a process where the received message is converted in to understanding. It is not necessary that the message reached to receiver will be understood by the receiver but decoding is a process which converts the message in to understanding. There are chances of misinterpretation of the massage.

- **Feedback** : This is the last part of communication process. After receiving the message, the receiver reacts or responds to the sender. The response can be based on the perfect understanding of the message or it can be based on the misunderstanding or misinterpretation of the message. This reply from receiver to sender is called feedback. Feedback has its own importance as the success or failure of communication is decided by feedback only.

3. TYPES OF COMMUNICATION

Communication in an organization may be either external or internal. **External communication** concerns with correspondence with those outside the organization. **Internal Communication** is concerned with communication within the organization. Internal communication can be classified into different communication like Downward, Upward, Horizontal, Grapevine.

Formal Communication : Downward, Upward, Horizontal, Diagonal Communication is formal communication. In this type of communication, information, circulars and notices are passing through levels in a formal style.

(1) Downward Communication :

Downward Communication starts from higher authority to downward authority, like the board of directors-managers-assistant manager-purchase officer-executive-clerk etc. It is a convenient channel to explain policies and organizational procedures / to appraise the subordinates for their performance. Major decisions are conveyed through this type of communication. Downward communication is too much authoritarian process where subordinates do not get any opportunity to participating in the decision process. It is a time consuming process.

(2) Upward Communication :

Upward Communication starts from bottom level to top level. For example, worker conveys message to production manager, he conveys it to the director of company etc. Upward communication provides necessary feedback. Upward communication is also important for workers' suggestions for the welfare of an organization. Upward communication is difficult as it moves upward against the force of gravity - means workers hesitate to initiate for upward communication. Workers at the lowest level are not efficient communicators so their communication oral or written may not be accurate and may not be welcomed by superiors.

(3) Horizontal Communication :

Horizontal communication refers to the flow of communication among the people at the same level of authority. The main objective of horizontal communication are developing team work and promoting group coordination within an organization.

(4) Diagonal (or Crosswise) Communication :

Communication between departments or employees in the same organization without any hierarchy is called diagonal communication. It is the most used channel of communication. Workers communicate with other workers, clerks sharing information with one another, managers discusses some organizational problems are all engaged in diagonal communication. Diagonal communication is extremely important for promoting, understanding and co-ordination among various departments.

Informal Communication : Informal channels transmit official news through unofficial and informal communicative interactions known as the 'grapevine.' This informal communication network includes tea-time gossip, casual gatherings, lunch-time meeting and so on. Grapevine communication is the best example of Informal Communication

(4) Grapevine Communication :

An informal channel of communication in an organization is called Grapevine For example people working together take interest in one another and talk about appointments, promotions, demotions or even domestic and romantic affairs of another. It follows no set lines or any definite rules but spreads very fast in any direction. Grapevine Communication provides much needed release to emotions. One of the major limitations of the grapevine is that it may spread baseless news which may harm the employees.

Grapevine Communication is not always negative for an organization and can be helpful because it helps in positive group building. It may help in building up organizational solidarity and harmony. It provides much needed release to emotions. Any information in the name of 'secret' spreads very fast. It provides feedback for management.

4. LEVELS OF COMMUNICATION

Human communication takes place at various levels:

(1) Extrapersonal Communication

(2) Intrapersonal Communication

(3) Interpersonal Communication

(4) Organizational Communication

(5) Mass Communication

1. Extrapersonal Communication :

It is a communication between human beings and non-human beings. This requires perfect coordination between sender and receiver. When your pet dog comes to you wagging its tail; as soon as you return home is an example of Extrapersonal communication.

2. Intrapersonal Communication :

This communication occurs within the individual's brain in the form of internal dialogue. For example when you "feel hot", the information is sent to brain and you may decide to "turn on the cooler", responding the instructions sent from brain to hand. Here relevant organ is sender, electrochemical impulse is message and brain is receiver. Next the brain assumes the role of sender and sends the feedback that you should switch on the cooler. So this process can be termed as intrapersonal communication.

3. Interpersonal Communication :

It is a sharing of information among people. It includes a few participants who are close to one another. Here many sensory channels are used and immediate feedback can be obtained. This can assume in the form of face to face conversation, video conferencing. and telephonic talk and soon. It takes place in our day to day life.

4. Organizational Communication :

Communication in an organization takes place at different levels. It may be upward, downward, diagonal and grapevine. This kind of communication can be divided into:

(a) Inter-operational Communication contains the structured communication within the organization.

(b) External – operation Communication deals with people and groups outside the organization. It is the organization's communication with its public – its suppliers, customers and general public.

(c) Personal Communication : Communication that occurs without purpose as far as business is concerned is called personal communication.

5. Mass Communication :

There are several mass media such as journals, television, newspapers, internet which mediate such communication to the large audience. Information in the oral form requires equipment such as microphones, amplifiers and information in the written form requires electronic or print media.

5. OBJECTIVES OF COMMUNICATION

Information

The main objective of a business is to pass on information and making people more informed, E.g.- all the advertisement activity that we see around as are an attempt to inform and pass the information on to others, and in case of business houses this information is mostly about the product or services that they have to offer. But the mode of communication may be verbal, written, visual or any other.

All business houses flourish on information relevant to their business activity. They must have good knowledge about the market, their competition, the government rules, the kind of credit that they can benefit from; the current economic position etc. Relevant information is the key to successful business.

But now in the modern times due to the advent of the World Wide Web, there has been a sudden explosion in the volume of information that is available to a business house and it is becoming increasingly difficult for a business house to find information that is reliable, complete updated and fresh. And it has become vital for any business to obtain that information. And this demand for accurate information has given birth to a new group of people called the infomederies, who do not deal with any kind of goods but deal in information.

Now a business house not only takes information but also give information, for e.g.- It has to give out information regarding profitability, the quality of products, the facilities that they provide to the worker or the services that they render towards the community.

Motivation-

Communication in business is also necessary to increase the motivation in the workers. So if the communication is done properly and is successful in motivating the workers and workers are motivated enough the work gets done easily, efficiently and they will work independently and with out supervision.

Communication should be used to create a right working environment. So that there is a healthy competitive environment among the workers and also that they can be recognized and rewarded for their achievements.

Employees working at a lower level in the hierarchy of the organization should be encouraged to provide suggestion and inputs on how to improve the working of an organization, this type of communication creates a sense of participation and belonging, it also develops more loyalty towards the company.

Raising Morale

Another very important objective of business communication (internal) is to keep the moral of the workers high so that they work with vigor and confidence as a team. This is a major factor that can have very serious impact on the success of a business house.

But as morale is a psychological factor the state of high morale is not a permanent factor. An organization may have a high morale among the workers for a quarter but may find that the employees have lost their morale in the next quarter. So to keep the moral of employees high an organization has to put continuous effort in that direction. It can be done by maintaining an open door policy, keeping an eye on the grapevine and not allowing harmful rumors to spread.

Order and instructions –

An order is an oral or written command directing the start, end or modifying an activity. This form of communication is internal and is carried out within a business house. Order may be written or verbal. Written orders are given when the nature of work is very important or the person who would perform the task is far away. We should always be careful while handing out written orders and should always keep a copy of the order so that follow up action can be taken.

Oral orders are given when work is of urgent nature and the person is nearby. But in both the cases it is very essential to follow up.

Education and Training

Now communication can also be used in business to increase the circle of knowledge. The objective of education is achieved by business communication on three levels (a) Management (b) employees (c) general public

(a) Education for future managers- Here junior personals in the organization is trained to handle important assignments involving responsibility, so that they can succeed their superiors in the future.

(b) Education for newbie's- When new personals join an organization they are inducted by educating them about the culture of the company, code of discipline, work ethos etc. This is usually done through a training mode to acquaint the new recruits with the functioning of the organization.

(c) Educating the public- Now this is done by advertising, informative talks, newspapers, journals. And this is done to inform the public about the product, the functioning of the company, and various schemes offered by the company.

6. GENERAL COMMUNICATION AND TECHNICAL COMMUNICATION

Technical communication is the process of conveying technical information. It is the process of communicating a specific message to a specific purpose. Technical communication is an exchange of technical ideas and information, knowledge and experience through writing, speech or by adopting. It includes simple definitions and descriptions of tools and machines and interpretation of principles which they follow scientifically.

Technical communication
- Always factual.
- Formal elements.
- Logically organized and structured.
- Specific audience.
- Complex and important exposition techniques.
- Usually involves graphics.
- Always formal in style.
- Technical content.
- Objective in nature.
- Special vocabulary.

General communication
- May not be always factual.
- No formal elements.
- Not always structured.
- Not always for a specific audience.
- No specific exposition techniques required.
- May or may not involve graphics.
- Both formal and informal in style.
- General content.
- Both objective and subjective.
- General vocabulary.

IMPORTANT ELEMENTS OF TECHNICAL COMMUNICATION

The important elements of technical communication are as follows :

1. Nature of the audience is considered

2. Content can be such that it can be understood clearly.

3. Audience needs are satisfied by providing the information in appropriate form

4. Some authors may be devote themselves for writing technical communication. Technical writing consists of aim of the audience, collection of required information, organization of information, Preparation of the first draft, Revision and editing of writing

5. Technical communication is created with a particular aim.

6. Technical writing includes project proposals, technical manuals and guides.

IMPORTANCE AND NEED FOR TECHNICAL COMMUNICATION

❖ Technical communication is the soul of organizational life It not only makes professional interaction possible but also directs the flows of technical information and knowledge for the guidance of technocrafts, engineers and others in their professional activities.

❖ The whole world has become a global market and the transfer of technology is playing an important role in economic growth and transformation. As the professional world becomes more diverse, competitive and result oriented, the importance of technical communication skills continues to increase.

Revolution in information technology creates a profound impact on technical communication tasks. These skills will be required in the changed technological environment. These skills include knowledge of high tech communication capabilities, ability to present and explain complex technical information, capability to understand and explain quantitive data, cultural awareness, capability and ability to analyze and priorities information

7. LANGUAGE AS A TOOL OF COMMUNICATION

Language is a combination of words to communicate ideas in a meaningful way. Effective communication is made possible with the help of language. By changing the word order in a sentence, you can change its meaning, and even make it meaningless.

Characteristics of Language

(1) Language is Artificial : Language is created by human being. It is not natural and original which was existed with the origin of the earth . It is created by human and for human. Every word is connected with every object / idea/thought. But the name of that object is given by human. (If we pronounced chalk stick as a donkey during its invention, then it might be known as "Donkey") So, Language is artificial.

(2) Language is Restricted : Sometimes we cannot express ourselves 100 %. When we converts our idea into speech, some meanings are lost in that procedure. That is the reason why we say that we don't have words to express ourselves. Language has limitations.

(3) Language is Abstract : Language s generalized ideas of things or thoughts. Any object of any shape, any sub-type can be known as same name. A 'table' can be of different shapes and sizes, and still be called a table. A "T-shirt" of any size (M,L,XL,XXL) can be called T-shirt. There is one general abstract name for each object.

(4) Language is Repetitive : Any language has characteristic of repetition and redundancy. This may make or destroy the communication. For example , We can say "Bell rings Tan Tan Tan ...." Moreover excessive and unnecessary repetition may lead to verbosity. If we say, "Bell rings Tan Tan Tan Tan Tan Tan Tan Tan , then it sounds awkward."

(5) Language is Recursive : Recursive means doing something with same method and same procedure. Language is like this. We can create different sentences and speech by using same Grammar rules and Vocabulary. Like in English, we have subject , verb and object. And we can make various sentences by using Subject, Verb and Object. In short, you don't have different rule for different sentence.

8. BARRIERS TO EFFECTIVE COMMUNICATION

A biblical story of "Tower of Babel" is a fine example of the breakdown in communication.

The word "Babel" is derived from Hebrew word "Babel" means "Confusion". In the biblical story of the Tower of Babel, the people of the world come together to build a tower that would reach heaven. These people were speaking same language. To break their pride, God has created many languages and People got confused with many different languages. Because of this, their communication results in breakdown of coordination. Intended message is frequently miscommunicated, misunderstood, misquoted or even missed altogether because of ineffective interpersonal communication skills.

THE PURPOSE OF COMMUNICATION

The purpose of communication is to get a definite response. In other words, he must be interested in the message, and he must accept it. There are several things which can prevent the message from reaching the target (Receiver). Communication is effective only if it creates the desired impact on the receiver through verbal and non-verbal mode. But many elements cause hindrances in its effectiveness.

EXTERNAL OR MECHANICAL OR ORGANIZATIONAL BARRIERS

(a) Defects in the channel : Defects in the devices used for communication are purely external; and usually not within the control of the parties engaged in communication. The telephone, the postal system, the telegraph, the loud speaker and other channels may break down or suffer from disturbance and may not convey the message properly. A partial failure of the mechanical equipment is more dangerous than a complete failure, because a partial failure carries an incomplete or distorted message, which might cause a wrong action to be taken. The postponement .of transmission, or communicating by an alternative method, is the only way to overcome the barrier.

(b) Noise :   Any interference in the message sent and message received leads to the production of "noise". Noise here does not mean cacophony, but a break in the communication process. The term communication barrier is an expansion of the concept noise. A noise is a break in the communication process.   Even in face-to-face communication without a microphone, the air may be disturbed by noise in the environment such as traffic, construction work, or human sounds in the neighborhood; organizations which can afford soundproof rooms can overcome this barrier. Communication by word of mouth has to be kept to the minimum in a factory because of the noise of the machines.

(c) Defects in the Organisation and Communication System :

Within the organization, the movement of papers and of information may be held up by the system itself. Orders and information which have to pass through too many levels of authority are often delayed. They are also likely to be distorted, because, at each level, they are edited, interpreted and explained before being passed on. This can result in communication gaps. In downward communication, the loss of information is said to be so great that many employees at the lowest level receive only 20 per cent of what they should get. One of the reasons for this is, too much dependence on written communication. Circulars, bulletins, notices and even letters are not read carefully. Many employees even when they are literate are unable to read and understand long messages. Even among better educated employees at higher levels, all written communication does not receive the attention that it should.

PSYCHO-SOCIOLOGICAL/ INTRAPERSONAL BARRIERS

Most of the psycho-sociological barriers discussed below operate at the emotional level.

Self-centred Attitudes : We tend to see and hear everything in the light of our opinions, ideas and views. We usually accept what agrees with our views, and reject or forget what goes against our opinions. We may even fail to perceive something that goes against our long-cherished opinions, ideas and attitudes. The attitudes may come from religion, nationality, ideas of the community to which one belongs, place of living or family ideas. These views form a frame of reference which colours every message, received or transmitted.

Group Identification : Our values and opinions are influenced, in some matters, by the group to which we belong. All persons have a sense of belonging to a group; we belong to many groups; for example, family, the larger family of relatives, our city, our religion or language group, age group, nationality, locality, club, economic group etc. An idea which goes against the interests of the group may be intellectually understood but may be emotionally rejected.

A bank or railway employee may understand the economic and political damage which a strike will cause to his country. Nevertheless, he does not accept any suggestion or persuasion that he should not join a strike because the ideas of his p are more important to him. Moreover, he may be afraid of being separated from his own group. So he cannot accept any communication which is against the strike.

Snap Reactions : A listener or reader may quickly or prematurely resond to the message because he/she is hot tempered. Such reactions are called as 'snap reactions.' They may prove to be barriers to communication.

Status Block : A "boss" often finds it difficult to receive favourably, any communication from his subordinates. People in senior positions often develop the feeling that they know everything about how to run the business. They do not realise that a junior may have something useful to say about the business. Many good ideas go unheard and are wasted only because they originate with junior employees who are considered to be too young and inexperienced to offer any useful suggestions. The ideas of workers are most likely to be unheard because of the social distance between them and the managers. A subordinate's nervousness in facing a much higher superior may prevent him from being attentive to words.

Closed Mind : Limited intellectual background, limited reading and narrow interests cause a person's mind to be narrow. This limits his understanding of human nature and makes him incapable of receiving communications with sym-pathy. This becomes a serious barrier to receiving grievances and appeals.

Wrong Assumptions : Many barriers stem from wrong assumptions. Wrong assumptions are made because the sender or the receiver does not have adequate knowledge about each other's background or entertains certain false notions. A skilled communicator keeps these issues in mind to prevent them from becoming barriers.

Poor Communication Skills : Lack of skill in writing and speaking obviously prevents the Tx from encoding his ideas properly so as to get across to his audience. Both these skills can be developed by training and practice. A business executive has to master the art of speaking to big and small audiences and also on the telephone. He must also be able to draft clearly and quickly. Nervousness in facing an audience may cause a speaker to speak poorly.

State of health : Physical condition can affect one's efficiency both as Tx and as Rx. It is common experience that a person in pain or fever is not inclined to engage in communication; but even when there is no pain or fever, if the state of health is poor, communicating ability is reduced because the mind is not sufficiently alert; there may be gaps in attention while reading or listening; there may be lack of energy to think clearly and to find the right words. Perception is low when the state of health is poor; and emotions which play an important part in successful communication, are easily disturbed. It is not advisable to attend to important communication tasks when one's health is not at its best.

SEMANTIC/LANGUAGE BARRIERS

Language is our most important tool of communication; First of all, words have multiple meanings; for example, a reference to the Random House Dictionary will show that the word "stall" has twenty-five meanings, including technical meanings used in specialised activities; similarly, the words charge, spring, check, suit, ring, have several meanings. Words in hindi like "Peti" , "Khokha","Sopari" indicates words connected with crime world. Words like minute and wind are pronounced in two different ways to mean two entirely different things. Even a concrete noun like table may suggest a statistical table, a' writing table or a dining table; and chair could be something to sit on, or a position to occupy. Phrases can be more tricky; a red and a blue carpet means two carpets, while a red and blue carpet is one carpet in two colours. Hence it is said, "meaning is in people, not in words." Jargon and technical terms are limited to the group of persons who work together, or work in the same kind of occupation; they need to use technical terms which have special meaning and describe a process in their work.

CULTURAL (CULTURAL VARIATIONS) BARRIERS

Any language is the expression of thoughts, feelings and experiences in terms of cultural environment. The same language when used in different cultures, takes a different colour and conveys a different meaning. Sometimes, we modify our language according to person with whom we are speaking. There is a difference in the use of language for discussions, formal talks, informal talks etc. Language influences the behaviour individual and groups.

HOW TO OVERCOME COMMUNICATION BARRIERS

Mechanical barriers are mainly in the form of defect or failure in the mechanical that are used for sending messages. The sender has to take proper precautions to see that devices such as telephones, fax-machines, cell phones, computer, radios, loud speaker, microphones, TV sets, mobile phones , etc. are in proper order and would not create disturbances while in use. Even traffic noise, loud conversations, etc. should be avoided as far as possible. Organisation which can afford sound proof rooms can overcome this barriers.

- To overcome defects in the organization and communication system, the system of internal communication has to be checked constantly to make sure that there are no undue delays in the passing on of information. In an emergency, an urgent message may be communicated by an alternative system.

- Physical barriers are mostly related to physical shortcomings or drawbacks. Sleeeplessness, fatigue, overworking etc may not permit the sender of message to convey what he desires in a proper way. The sender of the message should ensure that he is in proper health and physical order to function as the sender of the message.

- The personal barriers can be overcome only by making conscious effort to learn better methods and by training for better communication. Persons in responsible positions are expected to improve their communication skills and overcome their particular blocks. Many companies organise training sessions for their staff for better communication skills.

Suggestion schemes are meant to overcome status block. Some managers personally try to overcome it by developing friendly contact with their subordinates or by following an "open door" policy.

9. TYPES OF VERBAL COMMUNICATION

Communication by using language is called verbal communication. It is sub-divided into two : (a) Verbal – Oral and Written Communication.

ORAL COMMUNICATION

Oral Communication happens when we communicate with the help of spoken words. In this way, we can say that the conversations, meetings, conferences, interviews, training sessions, speeches, public announcements, radio speeches, telephone talk, public speaking, are all forms of oral communication. It can be used effectively to inform, satisfy, praise, criticize, please, inquire and for many other purposes.

Advantages :

- Oral Communication saves time.

- There is immediate feedback.

- (Oral communication saves money.

- In Oral communication, there is less formality.

Disadvantages :

- Oral Communication can be misunderstood more easily compared to written communication.

- If we consider the legal point of view, oral communication has little value as there is no permanent record or proof of what has been said.

- Oral Communication requires a good speaker otherwise it will not be meaningful.

WRITTEN COMMUNICATION

Written communication is also a type of verbal communication. With the help of writing, we express ourselves. The human language is expressed by means of visible signs. Since long, letter writing is considered the only reliable means of communication. Far a long time in the business world, it was believed that sending letters, memorandum and notices was the only proper way for businessmen to communicate.

Advantages :

- Written messages are less likely to be misunderstood and the doubts can be removed by reading it again.
- Written communication is best for legal or financial matters. It acts as a proof.
- Written communication has provided a permanent record. It can be preserved for years.

Disadvantage :

- Written communication is slow and time consuming.
- There is no immediate feedback.
- Written communication needs stationary and many equipment.
- Written communication is formal. It is only for literate people.

10. NON-VERBAL COMMUNICATION

Communication without using words is non-verbal communication. Basically there are two components of non-verbal (wordless messages) communication.

(I) Kinesics Communication
(II) Meta Communication

(1) **Kinesics Communication** : Kinesics communication is a message conveyed through non-verbal acts in the form of body movements such as gestures, winking, smiling, style of dressing and grooming. This type of communication transmits the unstated feelings, attitude and hidden intentions of the speaker.

(II) **Meta Communication**: Meta communication includes a message communicated not through words, but along with words. It conveys an implied meaning by the selection and tone of words.

COMPONENTS /FORM OF NON-VERBAL COMMUNICATION (Kinesics)

(1) **Facial Expressions** :   It is normally observed that the people from all over the world, even if they speak different languages, use a common pattern of facial expression to show emotions. Facial expressions are a complex matter and include eye contact. Smiling, frowning, raising eye-brows, etc. are universal in their nature and application. The facial expressions are used to show the following emotions: happiness, surprise, fear, anger, sadness, determination etc. facial expressions have to be understood in proper manner by the receiver of the message.

(2) **Gestures** : A gesture is the movement of the hand, head or body to indicate an idea or a feeling. Gestures are similar to facial expressions as they also help to know the feelings of the other person. Gestures convey emotions and also convey definite messages or information. There are some common gestures which are used by us in

day to day life like, waving the hand to greet goodbye, upraised hand to request to remain silent, wagging the index finger, for scolding, pointing the index finger, to show the direction, moving the hand sideway to show refusal etc.

(3) Body Language : Posture is an important element in body language as it often gives idea of the personality of the person and tells us a great deal about him or her. From the posture or the way a person holds himself we can know whether he is confident, diffident; old, young weak or strong. Body movements and postures appropriate for one person may not be considered suitable for another. The style of walking and moving that we admire in a dancer may be unsuitable for a school teacher. The occupation and work of a person can affect his posture and body movements.

(a) Silence : Silence has its own unique language. A person can convey his ideas even with the help of silence. Sometimes, we are overcome by emotions that we cannot speak - our silence tells the other person of our strong feelings. Every good speaker knows the importance of the pause which is a short period of silence between words or sentences. The student, if he remains silent before answering, it means he is thinking about the answer.

(b) Signs and signals : Signs and signals become very important means of communication ion when the communicants do not have a common language. The language of signs and signals has a universal nature and they are being understood all over the world. Signals are different from signs and symbols in the sense that they are dynamic and require some movement. Thus, a traffic signal flashes green, telling motorists and pedestrians to move on. Coloured bulbs are used in most offices to show that room are occupied or that the peon is being summoned by the officer.

(c) Graphs, maps and charts : Graphs, maps and charts are other types of visual, but non-verbal communication. People in business communicate messages more quickly and more accurately by using graphs, charts and maps than by long wordy explanation. The chief advantage of this mode of communication is that information can be gathered at a glance. A graph is a diagram consisting of lines to show the variation of two quantities. A map is a drawing on paper that shows the position and size of countries, towns, rivers etc. A chart is normally used by teachers especially at the primary school level. Charts are. also used by workers and at the managerial level.

(d) Colours : Colour plays an important role in our lives , we use them as symbols. Colours are used to convey direct messages. Traffic lights turn red and green and in an operation theatre a red bulb is used to show that the theatre is in use. Christians use black clothes to show that there has been a death in the family. A while flag is used in the army to show that the troops have surrendered.

(4) Para Language : It is often observed that sometimes our body language says something else and we speak something else. For example, when an unexpected guest arrives at our house, we have to smile and say, " I am very happy to see you", but our body language does not mention so. This is the use of para language.

(5) Time and Space communication : Time is considered to be the most important aspect our life. We have to plan our time and work accordingly. Time Management has also become a part of our study. Sometimes. when we meet a person who is hard pressed for time, he may not allow us too much of time so we have to be brief and convey our message in the least time. We should be brief but at the same time, try to speak about the important points. The importance of time can never be neglected.

An element of space plays an important part in our presentation of our personality. When we set tip during a meeting, move towards another table, take a file, go to the mike and speak, the movements in accordance with the given space is important. At the time of talking to others we do keep some distance from the person who is standing in front of us. While talking to seniors we keep some distance. This care gives a special effect to our communication. Distance between lovers and old aged couples indicates whether they are married or not.

(6) Sign Language : Sign language is normally used for deaf and dumb when they do not understand our language. Their teachers make effective use of such language. Sign language is also found when sign boards are fixed on the roads, near schools, near hospitals etc. they are the way of communicating with people. A board of the hospital will give us the idea that silence is to be observed near the area. Similarly, the idea of having a school around, will give us the idea to drive slowly.

Advantages and limitations of Non-Verbal Communication :

(1) Non-verbal communication has to be observed carefully otherwise the idea or the presentation of the thought is wasted away.

(2) It is particularly good for people who are uneducated or who have less education.

(3) It can communicate small ideas but when the detailed message is to be given it may not be of much use.

(4) It can be understood instantly and instant response can also be obtained but it cannot be preserved and recorded for further use.

(5) Sometimes, due to cultural differences the same sign and signal may mean different thing to the person who is responding.

(6) Nonverbal communication clarifies the verbal message. This can be seen in a presentation. The speaker is verbally communicating and uses nonverbal visual aids to help the listeners understand more effectively.

11. COMMUNICATION ACROSS CULTURE

During the path of successful communication, 'culture' often becomes a challenge, as it influences our approach to problems and our participation in varied groups and communities. Culture indicates to group or community with which we share feelings and develop our understanding to see the world. It includes society and groups . If one defines culture in this way, we all belong to many cultures at once.

Cross-cultural communicational flexibility is a major requirement for successful communication in our modern world. In the global arena workplace we tend to minimize or even to ignore our cultural differences while mythologizing that they no longer exist. But this is a dangerous myth for it greatly heightens the potential for miscommunication. The first step in addressing it is to name and accept our cultural differences. we can never really `lose' our cultural identity but we can add on other identities. we can never really `lose' our cultural identity but we can add on other identities. We communicate through language, symbols, gestures and our whole bodies. But just as we are able to communicate through all these means, there is always the potential to miscommunicate, or send unintended or false messages. Much of the conflict we experience in our global `market place' today is due to the experience of unfulfilled culture-specific expectations. We can avoid the conflict by understanding what results cross-culturally, in other words by understanding what is `acceptable' and what is not, cross-culturally. This process begins with recognizing the sources and contexts of cross-cultural miscommunication.

Rules for Communication across Cultures :

1. Assume differences with similarities are proved. Assume other are different from you instead of assuming similarities until differences are proved.

2. Emphasize description instead of interpretation or evaluation.

3. Try to know the background of your recipient before sending a message of communicating.

30

4. Treat your interpretations as working instruments and carefully assess the feedback provided by recipients.

The purpose of cross cultural communication is to know how people from varying cultures mingle and communicate with one another. If we want to open channels for communication across cultures, we have to find out the different ways in which various groups within our society have related to each other.

12. CONCEPT OF LISTENING

"God gives us two ears but only one mouth, because listening is twice as hard as talking."

Listening is a process of receiving, interpreting and reacting to the messages received from the communication sender. Effective listening is an art of communication, which is often taken for granted and ignored. In other words, Listening is the ability to understand the encoded message. Listening require conscious efforts of interpreting the sounds, grasping the meanings of the words and reacting to the message. No communication process is complete without listening

Hearing and listening are not the same People may often use these words interchangeably. In fact, hearing is solely depends on the ears, is a physical act, everyone can hear without deliberate effort. Hearing is merely vibration of sounds on the ear drum followed by electrochemical response On the other hand listening requires voluntary attention and then making sense of what is being said.

13. TYPES OF LISTENING

Different situation require different types of listening. We may listen to obtain information, improve a relationship, gain appreciation for something, make discriminations or engage in a critical evaluation. Listening can be categorized mainly in the following types.

[1] Discriminative listening :

As the name itself suggests, discriminative listening is the most basic type of listening, whereby the difference between the sounds is identified. If you cannot hear differences, then you cannot grasp the meaning that is expressed by such differences. By being sensitive to changes in the speaker's rate, volume, force, pitch and emphasis, the informative listener can detect even minute and minor meaning of difference in meaning.

[2] Comprehensive listening :

When the listener comprehends the message in order to understand the full meaning, it falls into the category of comprehensive or evaluative listening. This type of listening results in to selection of the needed information out of the total information. Students should involve themselves in this type of listening. Comprehension listening is also known as *content listening, informative listening* and *full listening*. There are two other types of listening which are similar to Comprehensive listening.

(A) Evaluative / Critical listening:

Evaluative listening is also called 'critical listening' because we make judgments about what the other person is saying. We seek to assess the truth of what is being said, We also judge what they say about our values, assessing them as good or bad, worthy or unworthy.

(B) Biased listening

Biased listening happens when the person hears only what they want to hear, typically misinterpreting what the other person says based on the stereotypes and other biases that they have. Such biased listening is often very evaluative in nature.

[3] Superficial/Casual Listening :

When the listener pays no attention on the content of the message , it becomes superficial listening. The uninterested listener can concentrate on the theme of the conveyed message.

[4] Appreciative Listening :

When the listener listens something for enjoyment and pleasure such as songs, jokes, anecdotes, stories, it becomes appreciative listening.

[5] Focused Listening :

When the listener listens something in the form of information, it becomes focused listening as the listener pays full attention to the content. Railway announcement, Reading of notices in school and college are examples of focused listening

[6] Attentive Listening :

In this type of listening, the listener's complete attention is must especially in situations such as interview, meeting, group discussionetc. Here the listener is expected to pay attention not only central idea but also to supporting as examples and illustrations.

[7] Empathetic Listening and Sympathetic Listening

This type of listening leads the listener not only to understand the physical message but also to peep into the listener's state of mind,feelings and emotions. Here the listener has to understand the speaker's implied meaning and intention. Psychiatrists listening to their patients fall in to the category of empathetic listening.

In sympathetic listening we care about the other person and show this concern in the way we pay close attention and express our sorrow for their ills and happiness at their joys.

[8] Therapeutic listening :

In therapeutic listening, the listener has a purpose of not only empathizing with the speaker but also to use this deep connection in order to help the speaker understand, change or develop in some way.

[9] Dialogic listening :

The word 'dialogue' stems from the Greek words 'dia', meaning 'through' and 'logos' meaning 'words'. Thus dialogic listening means learning through conversation. Dialogic listening is also known as 'relational listening' because with the help of exchange of ideas while listening, we also indirectly creates a relation.

[10] Relationship listening :

Sometimes the most important factor in listening is in order to develop or sustain a relationship. This is why lovers talk for hours and attend closely to what each other has to say when the same words from someone else would seem to be rather boring. Relationship listening is also important in areas such as negotiation and sales, where it is helpful if the other person likes you and trusts you.

14. ACTIVE LISTENING AND PASSIVE LISTENING

It has been calculated that most people speak anywhere between 100 and 175 words per minute. We are capable of listening, however, to nearly three hundred words per minute. Listening is anything but basically a passive, neutral activity. But many active processes are taking place within the listener, so we can say that Listening is not a passive activity

ACTIVE LISTENING

(i) It is the process of converting an idea or thought into message with complete involvement.

(ii) Listener encourages the speaker to express his ideas enthusiastically by showing interest in the speech.

(iii) It is a two way process where listener plays an active role.

(iv) Active listener never neglects the physical aspects of the speaker such as appearance, expressions, and bodily movements as they are very helpful to convey meaning to spoken words.

(v) To encourage the speaker active listener responds non-verbally by rolling eyes, changing facial expressions, showing smile and in this way shows his keenness to listen.

(vi) Active listening leads to effective and sound listener-speaker relationship.

(vii) Active listener shows his thirst for knowledge and information by asking relevant questions frequently

PASSIVE LISTENING

(i) It is the process of just absorbing the message without any involvement.

(ii) The listener discourages the speaker by expressing boredom on his face.

(iii) It is a one way process where the listener plays no role.

(iv) Passive listener has nothing to do with these physical aspects as he wants to bring out no meaning from the spoken words.

(v) Passive listener also responds non-verbally by yawning and showing boredom on face and discourages the speaker.

(vi) No scope for listener-speaker relationship and in fact the speaker wants to avoid such listeners.

(vii) Passive listener wants the speaker to conclude as early as possible and thus no chance of building up rapport between them.

Advantages of Active Listening

Active listening gives positive results. It allows the speaker to improve communication because one side is aware of other's view point. Speaker tries to give his best presentation. It helps in acquiring useful information.

15. EMPATHETIC LISTENING

`Empathetic' is an adjective of empathy which means an ability to imagine and share another person's feelings, experience, problems etc. These feelings are nothing but a state of mind and one can bean empathetic listener only when he / she listens someone very actively. This type of listening leads the listener not only to understand the message in the physical form but also to peep in to the listener's state of mind, feelings and emotions. Here the listener has to understand the speaker's implied meaning and intention. Psychiatrists' listening to their patients falls in to the category of empathetic listening. Empathetic listening is paying attention to another person with empathy. [Emotional identification compassion, feeling, insight]. An excellent technique to help one do this is called "active listening'. Another technique is to ask how the person feels about the situation or perhaps feels. Empathy is not sympathy. Sympathy means "feeling for someone', empathy is "feeling as someone." The most important issue about empathetic listening in a classroom setting is when to use it. The general rule is that teachers have a right to teach and students have a right to learn. When the teacher and student can engage in a dialogue that does not violate their individual rights or the rights of others, then empathy is certainly appropriate. However when either a student or another person is attempting to engage in a dialogue that is disruptive and violates the rights of the teacher and or/students, then the teacher needs to be assertive and bring the class back to order.

Important Elements/ Guideline of Empathetic Listening

- Build the trust
- Be attentive while listening
- Do not hurt the speaker's feeling.
- Allow disputants to express their emotions
- Reduce tension
- Provide problem solving environment
- Understand emotion and feeling of speaker

- Show interest in listening
- Use body language while listening
- Use words like "I understand you' or "I see'
- Do not interrupt/interrogate/teach/give advice/rehearse in your own head.
- Use open ended question
- Be sensitive to emotions

16. TIPS FOR EFFECTIVE LISTENING

Being Non Evaluative

If you are an active listener your verbal and non-verbal behavior should suggest the speaker that he is being properly heard and understood. It should not indicate what you think about a person. The purpose is to communicate overlooking the qualities of the speaker. The behavior of the listener should convey the impression that you accept the person without making judgment of right or wrong, good or bad,suitable or unsuitable.

Paraphrasing (summarize)

If you wish to clarify a point, you can simply summarize what the speaker has said and enquire the speaker whether you have heard it accurately or not.

Reflecting Implications (suggestions)

In order to per sue the speaker (to motivate the speaker) to extend his ideas, the listener has to reflect eagerness and willingness to learn more by using expressions like nodding or through verbal means, thereby giving positive feedback. This technique is can used by listener to get more information from the speaker in the area of interest of the listener . i.e. to divert the speaker from his main topic.

Reflecting Hidden Feelings

Sometimes the listener have to go beyond the general feeling and contents of what is being said to unravel the underlying feeling, intentions, beliefs that may influence the speaker's words .This would make the speaker evaluated. Acceptance is conveyed more by listenersmanner and tone than by the words.

Inviting Further Contribution

In a situation where listener haven't heard or understood enough. The listener can respond with empathy and understanding, prompt the speaker to give more information. The idea here is to get a better understanding of the subject by asking questions. But the questions should be for seeking information not to interrogate or challenge the speaker

Responding Non-Verbally

Listener can portray his image as that of a active listener by adopting certain postures, and sending non-verbal signal which communicates the listeners interest in what the speaker is saying. This may include eye contact, Leaning forward towards the listener, head nodding. Listener can also use some receptive utterances like 'yes' 'un-hum' to indicate that message of speaker is being understood.

Motivate yourself to listen

Listeners should motivate their mind to listen to the speaker carefully. They should prepare themselves to listen to others willingly. Listening can not be forced or imposed on the person. Individual should know the value and importance of listening.

Respect the speaker

Listeners should have respect for the speaker . They should not underestimate the speaker's ideas and thoughts. Even if, the listener disagrees with some of the ideas of the speaker, they should show their disagreement positively

Remove Horn effect

Do not underestimate a person because he has couple of flaws in his behavior . Many people are like rough diamonds. They need to be understood carefully. The speaker ideas can be rejected or doubted by the listeners. However listener should nor insult or dislike the speaker .

Positive body language

Listener should maintain positive body language like nod of head, leaning forward, maintain erect postures, during communication .Moreover listener should not create any type of distractions by using unnecessary body language. Many listeners revolve pen, notebook, or any other object in their hand.

Do not Interrupt

Listeners should not interrupt the speaker unnecessarily. Many listeners have tendency to make remarks or comments during speech. Moreover many listeners repeat the words and expression of the speaker loudly

Improve your listening span

Listeners should get training for enhancing their span of active listening. Many a times, we have to listen to speeches or lectures for long duration.

Speaker's use of appropriate body language

Speaker should use positive body language. Otherwise Listeners will be observing these body movements and thereby neglect ideas and expressions of the speaker.

Voice modulation

The speaker should modulate his voice and use different tones while speaking. It creates interesting atmosphere in the audience and they pay more attention to the speaker . It creates an environment for effective listening

Use Simple style

Speaker should use simple expressions that can be understood easily by the listeners. The speaker should keep one thing in mind that he should speak to 'express' and not impress. Use of heavy technical words, may distract the speaker and affect the process of listening.

Listening should be taught as a skill

The art of listening should be given importance in school and college curriculum. The skill should be taught to students just like, speaking, reading and writing skills. There should be sufficient practice and opportunity to enhance their listening ability.

Effective listening at all level is very important for the successful running of an organization. Good listening skills make workers more productive. The ability to listen carefully will allow you to:

• Better understand assignments and what is expected of you.
• Build rapport with co-workers, bosses, and clients.
• Show support.
• Work better in a team-based environment.
• Resolve problems with customers, co-workers, and bosses.
• Answer questions; and find underlying meanings in what others say.

Effective listening helps in controlling rumors which helps in preventing damage to the reputation of the organization. Effective listening will improve the working condition and nurture harmony and unity among the workers and colleagues.

17. BARRIERS TO EFFECTIVE LISTENING

• **Environmental Condition :**

Environmental condition like humidity, temperature, atmospheres limits the listeners span of listening. Cloudy atmosphere may cause the listener to sleep.

• **Space Distance :**

Distance between the speaker and the listener from long distance may effect the listening process. If the speaker is speaking from long distance, the listener may struggle to grasp what the speaker is speaking. Some of the words may be misunderstood by the listener.

• **Omniscient attitude of the listener :**

Many people considered themselves as ' know all' men .They think that they have perfect knowledge of everything in the world. According to them listening to others is pure waste of time.. They are not listening to the speakers because they thing that they already know what he is going to say.

• **Infrastructure :**

Poor Infrastructure may effect listening process. Lack of proper ventilation, light, acoustics can act as a barrier to listening

• **Speed of the speaker :**

Speed of the speaker can act as a barrier to listening. If the speaker is speaking too speedily, the listeners have no other alternative left than watching speaker . The Human brain receives sounds at a specific speed. If this speed is not maintained properly, the listener's may get distracted.

• Speakers' Non-verbal communication :

Speaker's no use of facial expression, gestures, body language, eye contact and other factors can create barriers to listening. If the speaker relies only on verbal expressions, the listener will be tired of constant bombardment of words and verbal expressions.

• Voice and tone of the speaker :

The listener will feel bored and fade up to listen to monotones speech. If the speaker's voice is not audible, the listener may not listen to it attentively. On the contrary, many speaker's maintain amonotonous tone which irritates the listener.

• Lack of Factual Information :

Many Times listener do nor listen attentively and carefully because he does not find any factual information in the speech

• Language of the speaker :

If the speaker is using high technical jargon and difficult words, the listener will be clueless about the meaning of those words. They will try to find meaning of those words instead of listening to the speaker .

• Horn Effect in the Listener :

The horn effect is tendency to underestimate a person as bad in all the fields because he is bad in one of the field. The listeners reject and nullify the speaker's chance to speak for more amount of time because listeners dislike the speaker .

18. PURPOSE OF READING

According to the Webster, "Reading is thinking under the stimulus of the printed page." Or "Reading is a psycho-linguistic guessing game." When you read, you read the lines, read between the lines and also read beyond the lines. So reading is nothing but a decoding process.

Reading is a prominent aspect of communication process. It is a processing part of written communication. In written communication, the process of decoding is done through the reading of the message. While reading, one can decode the message and send for analysis. This decoding in reading refers to the process of changing the coded message into information. It involves understanding the written language, it requires the ability to recognize words, understand the definitions of the words, purpose of the words used and literal and contextual meaning of the word. The main purpose of reading is to decode the message which is written. There are different purposes for reading. We read many things in our day-to-day lives. Let us name a few of them:

- Newspapers and magazines
- Advertisements, leaflets, pamphlets
- Textbooks, novels, short-stories
- Letters, telegrams
- Recipes, puzzles, menus ,Cartoons, comic strips
- Articles, reports, legal documents
- Dictionaries, telephone directories
- Time-tables, maps, statistical graphs and diagrams etc.

We have just listed the different texts that we normally read witch certain definite purpose in mind. They are read either for personal interest, for pleasure, to acquire information or to participate in society. For you, as students, the purpose of reading is emphasized on either for interest or for pleasure and reading to acquire information and knowledge. Reading for interest of pleasure is usually fulfilled through reading fiction, while reading to learn is associated with informative articles. Reading for information may be both internal and external. When you read for necessary background information about what is going on within the company where you work, or within your group it is called reading for internal information. Reading for the information of what is going on in your field, but outside your own company is called External information. People's interest in reading is so varied, that any text could meet any purpose

19. SKIMMING AND SCANNING TECHNIQUE OF READING

There are different styles of reading for different situations. The technique you choose will depend on the purpose for reading. For example, you might be reading for enjoyment, information, or to complete a task. If you are exploring or reviewing, you might skim a document. If you're searching for information, you might scan for a particular word. To get detailed information, you might use a technique such as SQ4R. You need to adjust your reading speed and technique depending on your purpose.

Many people consider skimming and scanning search techniques rather than reading strategies. However when reading large volumes of information, they may be more practical than reading. For example, you might be searching for specific information, looking for clues, or reviewing information.

Skimming and scanning are two specific speed-reading techniques, which enable you to cover a vast amount of material very rapidly. These techniques are similar in process but different in purpose.

SKIMMING :

Skimming is a method of rapidly moving the eyes over text with the purpose of getting only the main ideas and a general overview of the content. Skimming is used to quickly identify the main ideas of a text. When you read the newspaper, you're probably not reading it word-by-word, instead you're scanning the text. Skimming is done at a speed three to four times faster than normal reading. People often skim when they have lots of material to read in a limited amount of time. Use skimming when you want to see if an article may be of interest in your research.

There are many strategies that can be used when skimming. Some people read the first and last paragraphs using headings, summarizes and other organizers as they move down the page or screen. You might read the title, subtitles, subheading, and illustrations. Consider reading the first sentence of each paragraph. This technique is useful when you're seeking specific information rather than reading for comprehension. Skimming works well to find dates, names, and places. It might be used to review graphs, tables, and charts.

SCANNING :

Scanning rapidly covers a great deal of material in order to locate aspecific fact or piece of information. Scanning is very useful for finding a specific name, date, statistic, or fact without reading the entire article.

Scanning is a technique you often use when looking up a word in the telephone book or dictionary. You search for key words or ideas. In most cases, you know what you're looking for, so you're concentrating on finding a particular answer. Scanning involves moving your eyes quickly down the page seeking specific words and phrases. Scanning is also used when you first find a resource to determine whether it will answer your questions. Once you've scanned the document, you might go back and skim it.

When scanning, look for the author's use of organizers such as numbers, letters, steps, or the words, first, second, or next. Look for words that are bold faced, italics, or in a different font size, style, or color. Sometimes the author will put key ideas in the margin.

Reading off a computer screen has become a growing concern. Research shows that people have more difficulty reading off a computer screen than off paper. Although they can read and comprehend at the same rate as paper, skimming on the computer is much slower than on paper.

20. TIPS TO IMPROVE COMPREHENSION SKILLS

Definition :

Reading comprehension is the process of constructing meaning from text. The goal of all reading instruction is ultimately targeted at helping a reader comprehend text. Reading comprehension involves at least two people: the reader and the writer. The process of comprehending involves decoding the writer's words and then using background knowledge to construct an approximate understanding of the writer's message. Reading comprehension is defined as the level of understanding of a writing.

Reading comprehension is also affected by the quality of the reading material. Some writers are better writers than others, and some writers produce more complex reading material than others. Text that is well organized and clear is called "considerate text," and text that is poorly organized and difficult to understand can be called "inconsiderate text." The more inconsiderate the text, the more work will be required of a reader to comprehend the text. Readers who do not have the background, abilities, or motivation to overcome the barriers presented in inconsiderate text will have more difficulty comprehending these types of texts. Students who had trouble learning to decode and recognize words often will have difficulty with reading comprehension. Students who struggle with decoding rarely have a chance to interact with more difficult text and often learn to dislike reading. As a result, these students do not have sufficient opportunities to develop the language skills and strategies necessary for becoming proficient readers.

Tips for improving comprehension skills:

Reading comprehension skills can be developed through practicing and by implementations of some important tips. To understand comprehension, one should read a fairly long portion of the comprehension. It helps to establish report with the central idea of it. Develop reading practice and try to read attentively every time. Never judge on the base of short paragraph or small part of comprehension but read entire section and if needed then scan it .Use the technique of Skimming and Scanning where necessary. While reading a comprehension, mark or underline difficult words, make points or highlight important words. This will help to involve you in reading process.

Recalling of paragraph is also very important. Recall the paragraph and find out the central idea and also find out the purpose of comprehension. For better understanding of a passage, large word power and language command requires. Reading skill can be develop through such tips and will make reader more conscious as out the reading ability. Reading skill of comprehension helps the student to understand their subjective books very well.

In short reading comprehension skill can he improved a by pain wading task. by researching topic. learn new words, improve your understanding, Test your determination, by concentration, by using techniques of Skimming and Scanning and by marking words.

Reading comprehension requires motivation, mental frameworks for holding ideas, concentration and good study techniques. Here are some suggestions.

Develop a broad background.

Broaden your background knowledge by reading newspapers, magazines and books. Become interested in world events.

Know the structure of paragraphs.

Good writers construct paragraphs that have a beginning, middle and end. Often, the first sentence will give an overview that helps provide a framework for adding details. Also, look for transitional words, phrases or paragraphs that change the topic.

Identify the type of reasoning.

Does the author use cause and effect reasoning, hypothesis, model building, induction or deduction, systems thinking? See section 20 for more examples on critical thinking skills.

Anticipate and predict.

Really smart readers try to anticipate the author and predict future ideas and questions. If you're right, this reinforces your understanding. If you're wrong, you make adjustments quicker.

Look for the method of organization.

Is the material organized chronologically, serially, logically, functionally, spatially or hierarchical? See section 10 for more examples on organization.

Create motivation and interest.

Preview material, ask questions, discuss ideas with classmates. The stronger your interest, the greater your comprehension.

Pay attention to supporting cues.

Study pictures, graphs and headings. Read the first and last paragraph in a chapter, or the first sentence in each section.

Highlight, summarize and review.

Just reading a book once is not enough. To develop a deeper understanding, you have to highlight, summarize and review important ideas.

Build a good vocabulary.

For most educated people, this is a lifetime project. The best way to improve your vocabulary is to use a dictionary regularly. You might carry around a pocket dictionary and use it to look up new words. Or, you can keep a list of words to look up at the end of the day. Concentrate on roots, prefixes and endings.

21. PARAGRAPH DEVELOPMENT

What is Paragraph ?

Paragraph is a piece of writing , constructed by several related sentences with one central idea. The central idea is the topic or subject of a paragraph. A paragraph is a number of sentences grouped together which deal with one topic or a single point. There is no rule for the length of paragraphs. It may be short or long according to the need. A paragraph consists of a single sentence or of many sentences. We can divide sentences of paragraph into three category.

(1) Dominant or Topic Sentence : Expresses the central idea of the paragraph

(2) Supportive Sentences : Develops the idea by expansion, explanation, by support, by illustration

(3) Minor supportive sentences : Support to the central idea by providing minor and additional details.

Topic Sentences and Supportive Sentences

Paragraph development consists of topic sentence and supportive sentence. A paragraph is the sum of total of topic sentence and supportive sentences. Any paragraph can be easily classified by topic sentences and supportive sentence.

1. Topic Sentence : Topic sentence means a sentence that expresses the main idea of a paragraph. The main idea of a paragraph is expressed by one sentence is called a "topic sentence". The purpose of the paragraph or the subject of the paragraph is clearly mentioned by a topic sentence. Topic sentence should be written in a simple manner. It should concentrate the theme of the paragraph.

2. Supporting Sentences : Supportive sentences play very important role in paragraph development. Proper balance of topic and supporting sentence is needed in an ideal paragraph. Supportive sentences support topic sentence. By small supporting sentences, the related explanation and information can be written.

Attributes of a Good Paragraph

Paragraph can create important document, reports, proposal letter etc. The writing should be precise, correct, purposeful, clear, concise and meaningful. The following attributes/techniques/tips will help to create a good paragraph.

(1) Unity : Unity plays major role in the development of paragraph. There should be unity of idea in the paragraph. Entire paragraph should be with central idea of the paragraph. For proper communication, writer should convey the message to reader. Unity helps the reader to understand the message very clearly.

(2) Coherence : Coherence means the logical relationship between the elements and the compositions. It maintains the information or supportive sentences written into the paragraph in logical order. A paragraph is the sum of total of topic sentence and supportive sentences. The writer should use proper words and should be arrange in logical order. Coherence is a very important feature of paragraph writing.

(3) Length : Length of a paragraph is a very important aspect of paragraph. Through there is no particular rule for length of a paragraph. Length should be between the two criterias. Writer should give proper length so that it conveys

(4) Adequate Development: Paragraph should be written with proper depth. There should be combination of topic sentence and supportive sentence. In paragraph, to give proper message to reader, writer should justify the topic sentence by writing appropriate and enough supportive sentences.

Types of Paragraph

1) **Narration Paragraph:** Narration paragraphs are most distinctively used in fiction. As such, they will contain all necessary components of action development: protagonist, setting, goal, obstacle, climax and resolution.

2) **Exposition Paragraph:** It's created in order to clarify or explain a problem or a phenomenon. Writing exposition paragraphs requires strict focus on evidence and objective language

3) **Definition Paragraph :** Definition paragraphs are used in order to explain the meaning, origin and function of things. They are used both in academic writing and in fiction.

4) **Classification Paragraph :** Writing a classification paragraph takes a slightly varied approach. Classification can be performed on multiple levels – semantic (comparing different meanings of things), linguistic (using vocabulary to show contrast), and more.

5) **Description Paragraph :** Preferably, description paragraphs should concentrate on action (verbs), rather than sensations (adverbs and adjectives).

6) **Process Analysis Paragraph :** It, usually, takes the form of a how-to paragraph which guides readers through a process or action to be performed

7) **Persuasion Paragraph :** Persuasion paragraphs require exhortatory and dynamic language. They are aimed at persuading others into taking a particular action or adopting certain point of view.

22. EFFECTIVE PRESENTATION STRATEGIES

Definition :

A presentation is the delivery of information on a predetermined topic that you have created for a particular audience. Presentation is the practice of showing and explaining the content of a topic to an audience or a learner. Generally presentation is arranged for an explanation of an issue, to bring general awareness among the workers, for teaching purpose, and to divert your target mass in particular direction. In short, presentation includes information, analysis, explanation and persuasion. Most formal presentation have following purposes: (1) Presenting facts and information. (2) Reporting status/ providing updates of a project (3) Explaining procedure (4) Scheduling a business activity/ task/ process (5) Examine result and analysis future task. (6) Negotiating (7) Target achievement/ Training (8) Assigning tasks (9)Testing processes for suggestion and reviews (10) Inspiring the listeners (11) Organizing business activities (12) Negativity management The purpose of presentation is generally to put forward the aims and objectivity of any given task.

Purpose/Objectives :

1) Academic presentation is a part of the learning process. It is important for student's life.

2) In business field, one may present or introduce a new product of the company, general management discussion, new sales plan and presentation of achievement of an individual or a company.

3) Generally presentation is arranged for an explanation of an issue, to bring general awareness among the workers, for teaching purpose, and to divert your target mass in particular direction. Presentation may be for collaboration, for problem solving, making a major decision ,for increasing audiences' understanding of a particular subject. In short, presentation includes, information, analysation , explanation and persuasion .

Important Steps of Presentation

Effective presentations should be targeted to meet the specific needs, wants and emotions of your audience. The speaker must understand level, expectations and capacity of their audience. The person making the presentation should have an idea about the need of the audience and their expectations from the presentation. This analysis may help the audience as well the background of the listeners, their age group, gender, social status, economic level, educational background, religion, language, political association, attitudes, beliefs and ideals.

(1) Analyzing Audience and Location :

Before presentation, it is necessary to understand audience's level , expectations and their capacity to understand. Audience Analysis will include knowing the audience, grouping them, and recognizing their needs and requirements. For audience, One should analyze the audience on the basis of these questions : "Who are they ? What are their expectations of the presentation ? What is their level of knowledge? How familiar are they with the subject? Why do they want to attend your presentation? " Mainly there are 3 types of audience groups : (1) Novice/ fresher (2) Intermediate/ Semi-literate (3) Expert/ Experienced . Location is also important to understand. Due to cultural differences, problem of accent /linguistics problem may arise

(2) Preparing Outline of Presentation

The outline of Presentation is helpful in planning the presentation. Presentation includes so many information. Good organization of content is essential for effective presentation. Arrange them into 3 parts : Introduction, Body, Conclusion. The presentation should be prepared in following format : (1) Title: (2) Purpose: (3) Introduction of the Topic : The introduction comprises greeting, attention line, subject, statement, quotation or a question. Introduction finally leads to the main body of presentation which introduces the central idea of the presentation in simple and direct language. (4) Structure of the presentation (Main point/ Sub point/

discussion questions/ summing up Second main point/ Sub point/ discussion/ Summary Third main point/ Sub points/ discussion/ objections/ justification) (The body of presentation contains the main or the central idea. (5) Conclusion : Speaker should conclude the presentation by reviewing the main points. (6) Summary of whole presentation. (7) Recommending future action. Outline means the logical order of the presentation contents. Presentation should be well planned and prepared and rehearsed repeatedly.

(4) Visual Aids :

Spoken words are ephemeral (temporary). But if the presentation has been made using the audio visual aids, it gives lasting effect. Audio visual aids

- Increase audience interest
- Illustrate key points
- Signal transition from one part of the presentation to the next Help listeners retain information
- Help you deliver your speech better

Visual aids also increase audiences' interest in the presentation.Visual aids helps audience to understand the meaning clearly and properly.

(a) Overhead Transparencies

Overhead projectors are used for screening contents during presentation, Transparencies are used for presenting ideas with the help of overhead **projector.** The projector has a heavy glass scene on which the film is placed. The image will be bright and enlarged.

- **Use larger & simple fonts**
- **Keep the transparencies neat and clean Show only required information**
- **Do not make it more colorful**
- **Use pointer to draw attention of audience Understand the operation of OHP**
- **Keep the notes also ready in case power failure**

(b) Power Point Presentations

PowerPoint presentation tool (Projector) is widely used visual aid during presentations. According to one survey conducted by Microsoft every day 3 million presentations are prepared on power point slides. Power point tools are easy to prepare, economical and transportable. You can use same ppt. again and again. These tools require computers, screens, projectors.

- **Check the multimedia & other devices**
- **Familiarize yourself with transition of slides Transfer your files to the hard disc**
- **Rehearse your presentation**
- **Keep the printed copy of your presentation in case of failure**

(d) Blackboard or Whiteboard

Chalkboards are the most traditional visual aids frequently used in the presentation. Chalkboards are inexpensive and enable the audience to make notes during the presentation. The presenter can write down his plan on the chalk board effectively.

- **Clean the board & check the markers or chalk sticks before writing**
- **Write in legible size of fonts**
- **Stand to the side as you write**
- **Do not face the board while talking to audience Keep the main points on board, in case required**

(e) Flip Charts

A flip chart can be defined as a pad of large sheet of paper fixed to a stand, containing useful information for the audience. Flip charts can be prepared in advance. They can be used again and again. Flip chart enables the presenter to follow the exact outline of the presentation.

- **Use different color markers**
- **Keep the number of pages Write in large letters**
- **Use only one side of the chart**
- **Wait for the understanding of the audience**
- **Preferable use two pads.**

Tips for using Visual Aids

1) Organize the visual aids as a part of the presentation Emphasize the visual aids
2) Talk to the audience not to the visual aids
3) Avoid blocking the listener's view of the visual aids
4) Do not switch over to other point quickly
5) Do not make excessive use of audio visual aids
6) Do not use too many lines or figures in one aid
7) Make it legible and visible from distance
8) Be familiar with basic operation of the electronic devises that you are using

Nuances of Delivery / Mode of Delivery

Basically there are four modes of delivery.

(1) Extemporaneous

Extemporaneous presentation is the most popular and effective method. It does not require detailed preparation but to look the main points and start in front of the audience. It requires best oratory skills. Here Extemporaneous presentation sounds natural and spontaneous so that speaker can establish rapport with the audience through eye contact.

(2) Manuscripts

It means the speech is written in a paper and speakers has to read only. It is simply presented by reading the passage only. It is the most easy way of presentation as there is no need to recollect any matter and no need to Manuscriptmemorize it. It is a permanent and accurate record of whatever you have to say. There is no chance of tampering with the facts and figures.

(3) Impromptu

It is an informal style of presentation. It is used for informal speech or at familiar group. It is an informal style of presentation. It is used for Impromptu informal speech or at familiar group. For example, at a formal dinner party you may be invited to deliver a vote of thanks. Don't panic and babble something in an unmethodical way.

(4) Memorization

This method of presentation is very difficult for most of us. Probably a handful of you can actually memorize an entire speech. This type of delivery Memorization stands somewhere between extemporaneous and manuscript presentation. There are chances of making dull presentation. The speaker gets flustered if he forgets a word, sentence, or a whole paragraph

Body Language in Presentation

Body language communicates without word but we generally communicate by nodding head, blinking eyes, shrugging shoulder, by hand movement, smile, and other physical activities. Personal appearance plays an important role in presentation. Gesture also communicates important message by the movement of hands, eyes, arms etc. Facial expression can convey the mood of the speaker, expression, reaction, feeling, anxiety, recognition, hesitation and pleasure.

(1) Appearance communicates how we feel about ourselves and how we want to be viewed.
(2) Gestures can add impact to your speech. Similarly an ungainly gesture can disturb the effectiveness of the message.
(3) The face is most expressive part of the body. A smile stands for friendliness, a frown stands for discontent, raised eyebrow for disbelief.
(4) Eye Contact Looking directly at listener build rapport. Prolonging eye contact tell audience to pay attention.
(5) Proxemics: The use of proper space/ distance is very much important for your presentation

23. GROUP DISCUSSIONS

Evaluative Components of Group Discussions

Group discussion is a systematic oral exchange of information, views, issues, problems, and opinions about a topic, or situation among members of a group who share certain common objects. Group discussion is a systematic and purposeful interactive process. Group discussion can judge the candidate, his ability of communication, personality, knowledge, convincing power and ability to manage organization. Group discussions can be arranged among 8 to 10 candidates in the time limit of 20 to 30 minutes .

(1) Subject Knowledge : Subject knowledge is very important in G.D. Wide knowledge on general topics, current affairs, can be achieved by newspaper, magazines, television. In group discussion the person is evaluated on the basis of how he thinks and not on what he thinks

(2) Presentation : Along with knowledge, the powerful presentation of knowledge is also required. In group discussions, an effective communication skill also plays an important role.

(3) Language : The selection committee observes the language proficiency, verbal expressions, vocabulary power, sentence structure and clarity of language. Yourlanguage should be accurate ,free from grammatical errors ,also it should be direct, clear, and precise.

(4) Logic, Clarity and Body Language : Discussions should be logical and clear in thoughts and expressions. The selection panel observes candidates appearance, frequency of eye contact, postures, gestures and facial expressions. Positive attitude and proper body language plays major role in G.D.

Techniques of Organizational Group Discussion.

Organization GDs are mainly carried out for decision making. Organization G.D is a planned discussion to increase an organization's effectiveness and viability. G.D. Making is a complex process as it includes opinions and inputs of several people.

(1) **Brainstorming Technique** : Brainstorming is a method for generating a variety of idea and perspectives. It is an uncritical method because criticism stops the free flow of ideas. A group of 6 to 12 people sit around table. The group leader states the problem in a clear manner so that all participants understand it . No criticism or evaluation or judgment is allowed.

(2) **Nominal Technique** : The Nominal group technique restricts discussion orinterpersonal communication during the decision making process. The group members are physically present but they operate independently. Members meet as a group, each member independently and silently write down his or her ideas on the problem. The group now discusses the idea for clarity and evaluate them. Each group member silently and independently rank-order the ideas. The final decision is taken based upon the highest aggregate ranking.

(3) **Delphi Technique** : Delphi technique is a more complex and time consuming alternative in a group decision making. It is similar to Nominal group technique except that it does not require physical presence of members of a group. In fact, this technique never allows the group members to meet face to face. The problem is identified and the members are asked to fill a series of carefully designed questionnaires for solution. The results of the first questionnaire are compiled at a central location, transcribed and reproduced.This step is repeated until a common consent is reached.

Guideline for Group Discussions

(1) No of participants required : There is no fixed rule or standard to decide the number of participants in a GD. However, it is generally agreed that thereshould be 8 to 15 participants in a GD.

(2) Seating arrangements : The seating arrangement should be made in such a manner that every participant can see and speak to each other comfortably. Allotment of Topic: Generally, topic in GD is debatable point. Any current issue of regional , national or global importance is selected as topic of discussion . In some situations, the participants are allowed to select the topic on their own.

(3) Time period of GDs : Generally GDs last for 25 to 35 minutes. There are many recruiters who conduct GD for only 15 to 20 minutes. The participants are supposed to conduct the group discussion in a given time period.

(4) Appointment of group leader : No participant is appointed as a leader in GDs . There must be one group leader in G.D.

Role Functions in Group Discussions

People play various role in a group. All the GD participants play different role in Group Discussion

• **Seeking Information** : The participants seek information by asking queries, doubts, and problems

• **Giving Information/ opinions** : GD participants play an important role in a GD by Giving Information/ judgment/ opinions about an issue.

• **Summarizing** : There are many participants who play an important role in summarizing GD.

• **Evaluating** : The participants evaluate each other's ideas and take appropriate decision

• **Coordinating** : Coordinating is a crucial to success in a group discussion. Many GD interactants play a role of coordinator or moderator.

The main role of a participant in a group discussion is to express logical views on the topic. It should be resulted into proper justification of a subject, evaluation of all the aspects, clear presentation and proper conclusion. Participant should analyze the topic on the basis of his / her knowledge, experience, and background. One has to take care of the subject matter, its contents and meaning. The Participant should try to lead the discussion from its beginning, mid part and finally towards its conclusion. It is also necessary to maintain eye contact, open mind and listen to other's views along with spirit of cooperation. Your cool polite but active role can speak a lot about you.

24. INTERVIEWS

Definition :

The term 'interview' is derived from a French word 'Intervor' which means 'glimps'. Through an interview, we get a glimpse of the candidate in a short period of time. An interview is a formal meeting in which a person evaluates or consults another person.

Interview can be defined as an oral tool or test a candidate is traits for employment or admission. It is a kind of meeting between two persons for the purpose of getting view of each other.

Objectives :

We are very much familiar with 'Interviews'. Generally interviews are for the purpose of job but apart from that, there are other possibilities also. In job interviews, the employer's aim is to know whether the applicant can be of service to his company, and the applicant's aim is to find out the suitability of the job. The purpose of an interview is clear as it is for gathering relevant data about a candidate for a particular job position, promotion or making a selection panel. There are other methods also for appointment or selection of a candidate like group discussion, written test and oral presentations but experts believe that interview is the best method to evaluate a candidate and to find out his experience, possibility of performance and knowledge.

For evaluation of a candidate, there are different types of tools used in interviews, like face to face conversation, meeting, telephonic talk, video conferencing between a candidate and the selection committee or by candidate's presentation. In modem time, through the medium of internet, written test and online interviews are also taken.

An interviewer has just one objective: to decide whether or not to make you a job offer. While the interviewer will examine your work history and educational background, your strengths and accomplishments will also be important criterion. He or she is also interested in evaluating your level of motivation, values, attitude and personality. In other words, to find out if you're the right person for the job, what your potential is for promotion and whether or not you will fit into the company environment. One very important aspect of interview is to find out the candidate who has right attitude to do hard work.

While it is true that an interview is an important screening tool for companies, it also allows you to learn those things you need to know about the position and the company so that you can make an intelligent decision about the job. Always approach an interview focused on your objective: to get a job offer.

Interview process has become very technological now a days. It also become very professional and systematic. The demand of professional candidates is increasing day by day. To find out a proper candidate is a responsibility of H. R. Department of a company. The Company appoints experts for interviews and gives them the task of finding suitable candidates. On the other hand, there is tough competition in the job market due to unavailability of experienced and qualified candidates. Expectations are very high in corporate world as they want to fight business competition and professionalism has grown up in the corporate world. So according to the need of corporate world, interview patterns are changed.

Tips for Interview

A candidate needs to prepare at various levels of the interview physically mentally and psychologically, the candidate needs to prepare himself to remain succesful in the interview.

The candidate should make the following preparations:

- Candidate should have a clear picture of the company profile and the nature of the job for which the interview is being held in detail.
- Analyse yourself as it is very important to know about own self before somebody asks us to "Introduce yourself'. One should be clear about one's personality, likes and dislikes, hobbies, knowledge, interest, engths and weakness.
- Express your accomplishment if you get a chance in interview process.
- It is very needed to express your achievements in academic professional or any other. Your selection can be based upon your achievements, so candidates should express achievements in interview process.
- Every job has a set of functions for special skill to perform it. Company may look forward for particular skill from candidate so analyse and express your skills in interview. v Candidate's efficiency can come out by the subject knowledge so revision of subject knowledge will help the candidate before appearing for an interview.
- Candidate should prepare the interview file with required documents like interview letter, original certificates, experience certificate, reference letter, photograph etc. The candidate should prepare himself in the following manner

Types of Questions generally asked in Interview

There are basically five types of questions. Candidates should be familiar with these kind of questions which are frequently asked in interviews.

(1) Open Questions   In these types of questions, candidate canhave a space to speak about a topic or subject widely.

(2) Closed Questions Closed question means where candidate hasto give particular answer or there is no spaceto speak widely. Here, exact and accurate answer is required.

(3) Clarity Questions In this type of question, the main purpose of a Clarity question is to find out subject clarity of a candidate. Such questions can encourage the candidate to talk in detail about topic or subject.

(4) Suggestive Questions : In suggestive type of question, interviewer Suggestive can ask question to understand the candidate's   response clearly or in particular direction. It can be asked for confirmation. On the base of the early answers, interviewer can clarify the candidate's stand on a particular matter.

(5) Situational Questions :   In this type of question, interviewer can give a situation to handle to a candidate. The main purpose of this type of question is to judge the candidate's ability to handle difficult and sensitive situations.

Types of Interviews

With the changing time and requirement and with the arrival of latest technology, earlier pattern of face to face conversation of interview has been changed. The followings are types of interviews.

(1) Personal Interview :

- It is also called screening interview.

- The purpose is to decide through mutual information sharing whether a comprehensive interview is desired.

- In this interview, besides providing information about the job and the organisation, preliminary information is sought on past work experience, education and motivation.

(2) Patterned Interview :

- In this kind of interview what is to be asked is already structured and hence they are called structured interviews.

- Patterned interviews are a combination of direct and indirect questioning of the applicant

(3) Non-directive Interview :

- In this interviewing technique, there is a minimum use of direct questions.

- Questions that can yield 'yes' or 'no' answers are avoided, and instead broad general questions are asked in the interview. Such questions help in revealing the applicant's real personality.

(4) Stress Interview :

- It is a deliberate attempt to create tension and pressure to observe how an applicant performs under stress.

• Stress is created by not allowing him to complete his answers or too many questions are asked in quick succession. Some may react in a mature way by keeping their cool and yet try to answer the questions, others might lose them cool and react sharply such interviews as are useful in jobs where emotional balance is a key requirement.

(5) Behavioral Interview :

• The behavioral interview considers the candidates' past performance as the indicator for their future performance. The candidates are asked to describe their previous job profile and mention some instances where they played a major role in job-work.

• The candidate must be able to describe and prove his/her competencies.

• He/she should remember each and every aspect of his past job behaviours; the candidate must be able to relate any organizational competency with his/her own competencies.

(6) Depth Interview :

• The purpose of depth interview is to get total information on an applicant in order to develop a comprehensive profile based on in depth understanding of his personality.

• This kind of interview is usually very time consuming because a lot of time is spent with the applicant to get detailed information on various core areas of knowledge and skills of the job.

(7) Group Interview :

• It is a recently developed technique. It offers some promise for the appraisal of leadership but it lacks proper validity.

• A topic of discussion is assigned to the group of applicants and their performance is evaluated by Interviewervers.

(8) Panel Inteview :

• Interviewing candidates by a single person may not be effective as he cannot judge the candidates in different areas/skills. Hence most organizations invite a panel of experts, specialized in different disciplines, to interview candidates.

• The great advantage of this interview is that it helps to coordinate the collective judgment and wisdom of members of the panel.

(9) Telephonic Interview :

• It becomes very common today due to less availability of time and distance.

• Telephonic interview takes place in a traditional structure of questions on telephone.

• It is very useful as it saves time but it has weakness as there is no physical appearance of a candidate.

(10) Video Conferencing Interview :

• This is like face to face interview but possible for the candidate who is far away from the place.

• Through video, selection committee can ask different questions and observe behavior and non-verbal gestures of a candidate.

Importance of Non-Verbal Aspects in Interview

Non-verbal aspects have equal importance as verbal has. It conveys very important message to the committee in positive and negative way as interview process is very critical, non-verbal play very vital role in judgment of committee. Here non-verbal aspects cover appearance a candidate, self-confidence, Behavior, interview, fear. body movement, eye contact, attitude etc.

Positive behavior : Positive behavior is very important and along with verbal communication, it should be conveyed by non-verbal communication also. Candidate's politeness and attentiveness can be /elected by non-verbal communication. Even paralanguage indicates so many things.

Body Language : While appearing for an interview. it is very natural for candidates to be nervous. This nervousness reflex is in fast heartbeats, breathing becomes more rapid and mouth becomes dry. This type of nervousness gives negative impression of candidate to selection committee. It is even reflected clearly by body language of a candidate so non - verbal aspects play a very important role in interview,

Physical Appearance : Candidate's appearance is very important and gives positive or negative marks. The body language of gestures. movements and postures are called kinesics. Good physical appearance attributes highly positive features of individuals. On the opposite side, poor physical appearance tend to attribute negative characteristics of individuals. One important aspect that is eye contact which is one of the parts of body language. Eye contact varies with gender and with different cultures.

Rule of Touch : There are certain rules of touch that are considered to be acceptable in most cultures. Rules of touch are as important as all the other non verbal communication. With certain touches we can show our position inclination toward individuals while if not aware of certain rules of touch within a specified culture we may attribute a negative regard. Hand gestures are the most important of body gesture. Hand gestures can often convey a message of a ward or a sentence.

25. BUSINESS LETTER

Basic Parts of Business Letter

(1) **The Letter Head / The Heading / The Head Address** : The Letter Head is printed at the top center of the letter-sheet. Sometimes it is also written on the left or the right side of the letter-sheet. It consists of the name, the business and the address of the company. It also includes the telephone number, fax number, E-mail address, and website, if any. It also includes emblem (logo or symbol) of the company. The Letter Head should be simple and dignified. Most companies prefer a simple design in a single colour.

(2) **The Date** : Generally, The date is written two or three spaces below the last line of the letterhead. It is always on the right hand corner. The date consists of the date, name of the month and the year. The date is written in two styles.

(a) The British Method : 4th July, 2011
(b) The American Method : July 4, 2011

The British Method is also called the ordinal numbers method and the American Method is called the cardinal numbers method. The date should never be written like 7-2-02 or 7/2/02 because it shows that the writer is careless or in a great hurry.

(3) **The Inside Address** : The inside address is written on the left, beside the margin. It is written two spaces below the date- line. The Inside address contains the name and the address of the firm or the individual to whom the letter is written. Inside Address can be used to make windows envelope.

There are two methods of writing inside address.

(1) Indented Form
(2) Block Form

(4) **The Salutation** : The salutation is written beside the left – hand margin, two spaces below the last line of the inside address. The salutation is followed be a comma (,) or a colon (:). The salutation is a compliment or greeting used to begin the letter. Just as "Good Morning" is used to begin a talk. It is the written equivalent of the conversational "Hello". "Dear Sir" "Dear Medam" , "Respected Sir" is salutation

(5) **The Body / The Text / The Script of Letter** : The first line of the body begins two spaces below the salutation. It appears between the salutation at the beginning and complimentary close at the end. It is that part of the letter which contains the message or the information to be communicated. This is the most important part of the letter. The letter is divided in the following parts.

(1) Introductory paragraph
(2) Main paragraph
(3) Closing paragraph

(6) **The Complimentary Close** : The Complimentary close is written on the right two spaces below the last line of the body. It should not extend into the right hand margin. The Complimentary close is a polite way of saying " Good bye". Just as the salutation is the written equivalent of "Good Morning" or "Hello". So, the complimentary close is the written equivalent of "Good Bye" "Yours faithfully / Yours sincerely / Yours truly" is complimentary close.

(7) **The Signature** : The Signature is written just below the complimentary close , near the right hand margin. Sometimes , it consists of only the name of the writer.

(1) A sole trader will put his signature by writing his own name. (2) Any partner of a partnership firm can sign letter on behalf of the firm. (3) In big business houses, it is not possible for all partners or owner to write or reply all the letters. So, a responsible employee of the firm is given power to sign the letters.

Thus, the employee who signs the letter on behalf of the other is said to sign per procurationem (per pro). It means that such a person is legally authorized to sign letters.

Per Pro M. Patel and Company

Nitin R. Raval

The signature is proof that the person signing has written that letter. It help to pin point responsibility for the writing of the letter.

Tips for Effective Business Writing

(1) Business Letter should be clear and concise.

(2) While writing letter, one should keep in mind the reader's benefits and advantages for them. It is called "The You Attitude."

(3) The writer should set down the goal because it help him to decide why is he writing and what does he wants to achieve.

(4) While writing a business letter , one should use a friend tone but not at the cost of efficiency.

(5) Opening lines of business letter are most important because they are read attentively and carefully and conclusion should be courteous.

Letterhead or
typed heading

The Ohio Academy of Science
1600 West Third Avenue Suite 303
Columbus OH 43212-2817
Phone or FAX (614) 488-2228

Date

January 10, 1997

Inside
Address

Mr. John M. Smith
Chief Executive Officer
Smithville Corporation
123 Easy Street
Smithville OH 21234

Salutation

Dear Mr. Smith:

Body
(Text)

This is the first line of the first paragraph. It
should state the purpose of the letter or the reason for
writing. This may be the only paragraph that gets read. So
brief and clear. Write and rewrite until you get it right.

This is the second paragraph. Most letters have more
than one paragraph. Although your letter should be more
exciting to read than this one, it will not be well received unless it has all of the essential elements of a
standard business letter: heading, date, inside address,
salutation, body or text, complimentary closing, your
handwritten signature, and your name typed below your
signature.

Although there are variations to these basic elements, including additional parts for special purposes,
you can spend the rest of your life happily writing standard business letters if you get these basics right now.

I'm closing this letter now so that I can demon-
strate the final elements of a letter.

Thank you for considering these suggestions.

Signature

Sincerely,

Complimentary closing

Lynn E. Elfner
Chief Executive Officer

Typed
name

LEE:bgl

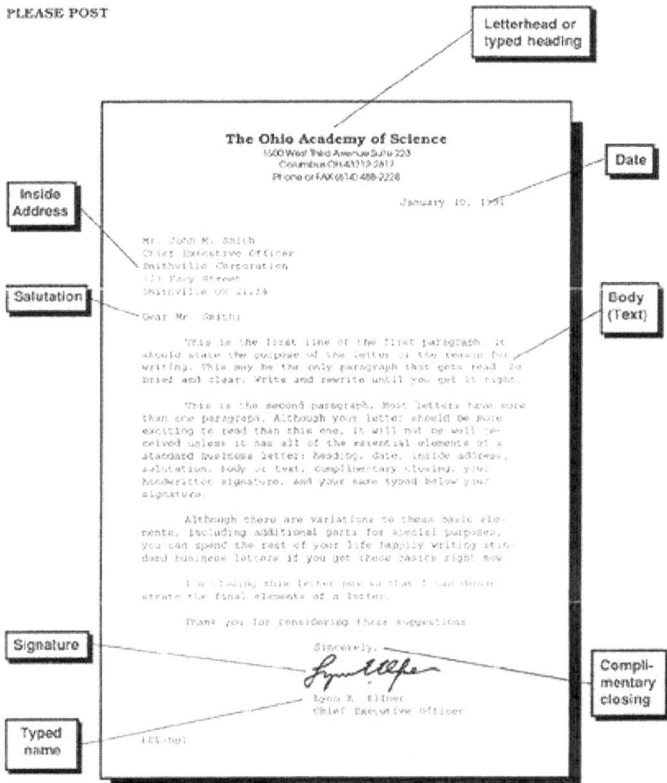

HOW TO WRITE A BUSINESS LETTER

Inquiry Letter

Inquiry Letter :   A person / a shop asks for certain information in the form of catalogue/price list/quotation /terms and condition / any inquiry. That letter is known as inquiry letter

(1) **Solicited Inquiry Letter** : You have seen an advertisement in newspaper. As a dealer write a letter of inquiry.

Dear Sir,

Sub : Inquiry for any item asked in question

(for example : table fan/dryer/ scanner)

We are very much impressed by your advertisement of…(any item)…… in Times of India. (newspaper). We are leading dealer of ……(any related business)……… in our city.

We want to purchase …(what u want to buy)……….. Please send us your latest catalogue and Price-list. / Please send us your competitive quotation / Please let us know about your terms and condition. As our order is large , we want maximum discount and favourable terms of payment.

If your terms and conditions, facilities and mode of payment are favourable to us, we shall place our order soon.

We wait for your prompt and favourable reply.

Thank You.

Yours Faithfully,

2) **Unsolicited Letter** :

As a dealer write a letter of inquiry without referring any advertisement .

Dear Sir,

Sub : Inquiry for any item asked in question

(for example : table fan/dryer/ scanner)

We have been dealing in the business ...(any related business).........since 1990. We have come to know that your company manufactures ....

We want to purchase ...(what u want to buy)........... Please send us your latest catalogue and Price-list. / Please send us your competitive quotation / Please let us know about your terms and condition. As our order is large , we want maximum discount and favourable terms of payment.

If your terms and conditions, facilities and mode of payment are favourable to us, we shall place our order soon.

We wait for your prompt and favourable reply.

Thank You.

Yours Faithfully,

Complaint Letter

You have received 100 damaged/defected goods / goods which is not matching with goods that you have ordered / goods which is less in quantity.

Dear Sir,

    Sub : Complaint for damaged /defected / wrong goods /shortage in quantity.

We have received the consignment sent by you against our order letter no. ………….. We thank you very much for the prompt execution of our order. However, we regret to draw your attention to the following complaint.

(1)   Damaged Goods : On opening the consignment , we have found …………… in a damaged condition. Our customers do not buy items even with single fault/damage. We have clearly instructed you to pack the goods properly.

(2)   Inferior Goods : On opening the consignment, we have found……………..to be of inferior quality. They do not match with the samples shown to us. There is no demand of this product in our area.

(3) Wrong Goods : On opening the consignment, we have found 100 Hero cycle instead of 100 Atlas cycle. We have ordered……………….. Please refer to our order.

(4)   Shortage in Quantity : On opening the consignment, we have found ...10 phone... less in number. We cannot ignore such a big shortage. Therefore we request you to send us remaining goods as early as possible.

(5)   Defected Goods : On opening the consignment, we have found .... in a defected condition. (Write any defect related to product). Our customers do not buy items even with single fault/damage.

•   We shall try to sell these items if you give us 20 % discount.

•   We request you to send new as early as possible.

•   We want to cancel our order and want refund.

       We wait for your prompt and favourable reply.

       Thank You.

                                                           Yours Faithfully,

Adjustment Letter

Adjustment Letter : Adjustment Letter is a reply of complaint letter by company which can suggest some suitable adjustment for your complaint (They may accept your proposal or They may reject your complaint. However suitable adjustment will be giving discount / replacement /sending goods as early as possible.

Dear Sir,

> Sub : Adjustment for damaged goods/defected goods /wrongs goods / late delivery

We have received your complaint letter dated on ....   We are sorry for the inconvenience caused to you.

(After this write down any investigation / inquiry / search you have carried out to find out cause of complaint or accept your fault by saying : " your complaint is genuine ")
For example :

• On inquiry, we have found that your complaint is genuine.
• On inquiry, we have found that the damage was caused because of mishandling of goods during transit.
• On inquiry, we have found that our packing department had wrongly shipped your consignment to other dealer and his consignment to your shop.
• On inquiry we have found that you haven't received the goods because of stirk/bomb blast. • Any Reason (Adjustment Letter) for causing damaged /defect/wrong delivery/inferior delivery/rude behaviour/late delivery
(After this , give adjustment or don't give adjustment)
• It is not our mistake. Hence we recommend you to ask about this matter to transporation. • We will give you 10 % discount.
• We will replace that good.
• We will send you the good as early as possible.
• If you want to cancel the order, we are ready to give your money back.

Our motto is to satisfy customers. We think our explanation will satisfy you and will continue your patronage. We assure you that you will not have to face any difficulty form us in future.

Thank You.

Yours Faithfully,

26. REPORT WRITING

Definition

A report may be defined as a formal document based on collection of facts, events and opinion and usually expresses a summarized and interpretative value of information. It can be defined as communication in which a person, who is assigned the work of report making, gives information to some individual or organization because it is his or her responsibility to do so. The word 'report' is derived from the Latin word – 'reportare' – means to bring back.

Types of Reports : Reports can be classified as follows :

(1) Formal and Informal Repots

(2) Routine and special Reports

(3) Oral and written reports

(4) Informational and Analytical Reports

Formal Report	Informal Report
<ul><li>A formal report is prepared in a prescribed form.</li><li>It is lengthy reports with length of hundred pages.</li><li>Annual Reports, reports of companies, project reports and thesis are examples of formal reports.</li></ul>	<ul><li>An informal report is generally in the form of a person to person communication.</li><li>It is brief report of a specific business.</li><li>Laboratory reports, daily production reports, trip reports are informal reports.</li></ul>

Routine Report	Special Report
• Routine reports are prepared and presented at regular intervals. • They may be submitted annually, semi-annually, quarterly, monthly, weekly and daily. • Sales and production report, cost report are examples.	• Special reports is prepared and presented to convey special information related to an individual ,occasion or problem. • Enquiry report, research reports, thesis, dissertation are special reports.
Oral Report	**Written Report**
• It is presentation of data in the from of face to face to communication • Reports of accidents, sales production, joining are example of oral reports.	• It is presentation of data/information in written form.. • They can be kept as permanent record / can be edited, reviewed and stored.
Informational Reports	**Analytical Reports**
• It is presentation of data/information without any analysis or interpretation or recommendations. Conference report, seminar report and trip report are example.	• It is presentation of data/information with analysis or interpretation or recommendations. Project reports, Feasibility reports, market research report are examples.

Format of Reports

There are four types of formats to write technical reports.

(1) Printed Format

(2) Letter Format

(3) Memo Format

(4) Manuscript Format

(1) Printed Format : It is written in the prescribed form by the organization. All one need to do is to fill in the blanks in this printed form. For example, sales reports, tour reports.

(2) Letter Format : It is a short reports of a few pages. Besides all routine parts of a letter, this type of format includes illustrations, footnotes, references and so on.

(3) Memo Format : A memo- memorandum format is mainly used for short reports to be communicated within organization. It is used to send from one department to another. It is short version of letter format.

(4) Manuscript Format : The manuscript format is generally used for long and formal reports. The length of such reports can be form few pages of hundred pages. The following is structure of manuscript format.

Structure of A Formal Reports in manuscript format :

The Title Page	It includes name and status of author, department and date of issue. The title of reports should be clear, short and unambiguous.
Acknowledgement	One should express his gratitude to everyone associated with assignment and preparation of his reports generously.
Letter of Transmittal	It covers a summary of finding, conclusions and recommendations to give an idea of the report.
Table of contents	It indicates the topics and their page numbers in the report for the reader.
Abstract and Executive summary	An abstract is short summary about 200 words while an executive summary is a more detailed overview of a report.
Introduction	It includes purpose, methods of inquiry, arrangement or grouping of data and general background to report's subject.
Findings	Finding presents the results of the investigation.
Conclusion	It states the results of the investigation. It offers answers to question raised in the beginning.
Recommendation	It is the action center of the report. It includes clear and definite recommendations.
Appendix	Appendix includes secondary or extra information. Tables, flow charts, maps are generally included.
Reference and Bibliography	All published and unpublished sources of information used in preparing the report are listed under Bibliography and reference.

Objectives of Reports

• To give information about the organization's activities, progress plans and problems

• To record events for future reference in decision making

• To recommend specific action

• To justify and persuade readers about the need for action in controversial situation.

• To present facts to the management to help decide the direction the business shouldchoose.

Characteristics of reports

Brevity	The writer or the report should use fewest possible words.
Accuracy	The facts presented in report should not only accurate but also relevant.
Clarity	A good report must be absolutely clear.
Reader Orientation	A good report is always reader oriented. It means the writer should keep in mind who is going to read it.
Objectivity of Recommendations	The recommendation must be impartial and objective.
Simple and unambiguous language	A good reports is a scientific document, it should be free from business jargon, figures of speech.
Grammatical Accuracy	A report must be written with grammatical accuracy for proper understanding.
Special Format	Technical reports use a special format like title page, acknowledgment, letter of transmittal, table of contents, summary etc.
Illustrations	A good technical report should be free of illustrations which may be tables , graphs, maps , drawings , charts and so on.

NEWYORK MILLS LTD.
AHMEDABAD (GUJARAT)
INTEROFFICE MEMORANDUM

Date	:	**20th December, 2008**
Ref.	:	**The Managing Director**
To	:	**Managing Director**
From	:	**A.M.Patel, Health & Safety officer**
Subject	:	**Inspection of company canteen**

On 15th December, 2008, I inspected the canteen of company and it was a roution one. I concentrated on two main aspects- hygiene and salty

1 Hygiene: I didn't find the standard of hygiene satisfactory. I discovered –

- Food left over from lunches is stored in the fridge
- Staff don't wash the crockery properly
- The fridge is not defrosted at regular intervals

2   Safety : Owing to overloading of the only electric socket in the

- Kitchen, staff is using the wall socket just outside the kitchen to boil water for drinks. The trailing flex from the kettle creates a safety hazard

Recommendations :

I suggest the following recommendations:
1.The responsibility should be given to every member in circulation
regarding hygiene and safety.
2. All the staff should be reminded that kettles one to be used only in the kitchen.

Yours sincerely,

A.M.Patel

ULTRA ENGINEERING LTD.
Phase-II, GIDC, Vatva,
Ahmedabad
www. meghmani.com

15th April, 2009

The Managing Director,
ULTRA ENGINEERING Ltd, Phase-II,
GIDC, Vatva,
Ahmedabad.

Dear Sir,
   Sub : Report on the Causes and Remedies of the Labour Problem at
   Our industry.

In accordance with your instructions given to me on 20th March,' 09, I submit here my report on the causes and remedies of the labour problem at our industry. Let me first expose the causes of the problem.

(1) Pay Scales: Because the prices of essential commodities are soaring higher day by day, the Employees' Union is demanding 15% rise in their basic salaries and 40% rise in Dearness Allowances. Their demand is based on the 2008 Report of the Wage Board for Engineering Industries, New Delhi.

(2) Bonus: Our employees are not happy with the 8.33 % bonus we are giving them. They insist that the rate of bonus should commensurate with the profits earned by our industry.

(3) Provident Fund, Gratuity and Pension Scheme: At present our employees contribute 8.33 % of the total salary to the Provident Fund.

(4) Amenitics : Our technical and non-technical staff demands that the management should provide certain amenities such as – Transport, Priamary and Secondary Schools, A Welfare Centre with a good library.

(5) Working Conditions : The employees are also dissatisfied with the present working condition . They want us to install air-condition machines where labour work is active. They want general cleanliness and proper ventilation

Recommendations

(1) Long Term Measures : The Board of Directors should invite labour leaders and convince them certain amenities cannot be given immediately. But let us assure them that their demand for Schools, Training Center and Hospital will be settled within a 5 year programme.

(2) Short Term Measure : Without further delay, the Board of Directors should have open-hearted negotiations with the labour leaders and try to settle their demand for a rise in basic salaries and Bonus.

I hope Sir, that my report will help you to solve the labour problem at our industry and solve it in a graceful manner.

Yours faithfully,

Chintan Mahida
(Secretary)

27. PROPOSAL WRITING

Definition :

A piece of communication – either oral or written which can persuade someone to accept the suggested views or ideas is a proposal. It is systematic, factual, formal and persuasive description of a course of action or a set of recommendations. A proposal is an offer or bid to complete a certain project for someone.

Types of Proposals :

Formal Proposals	Non-Formal Proposals
• Formal proposals are lengthy proposals. • It is written for big projects • It is written in manuscript format.	• Non-formal proposals are brief proposals • It is written for small projects • It is written in printed form, letter or memo formats.
Internal Proposals	**External Proposals**
• An internal proposal is for reader within an organization • It helps to study and solve problem of organization.	• An external proposal is for reader outside an organization. • It helps to study and solve problem of organization.
Solicited Proposals	**Unsolicited Proposals**
• A proposal written in response of a particular request from a client is known as solicited proposal	• Unsolicited proposal are written without any request for a proposal.

Purpose & Characteristics of Proposal

Purpose :

- ➢ To initiative a new project
- ➢ To provide fresh ideas
- ➢ To solve problems
- ➢ To reinforce innovative strategies
- ➢ To conduct the basic research before developing a new plan
- ➢ To modernize the office procedures of an organization

Characteristics :

- ➢ Proposals should be more creative in comparison of other forms of professional writing
- ➢ Proposal should contain a course of action with the rationale.
- ➢ Proposal should keep in mind the customer's convenience, financial benefit and prestige.
- ➢ Proposals look attractive and written neatly.
- ➢ Proposals should include background, objective , description , summary of the problem.

Structure of Proposal :

Title Page	It includes the title of the proposal, the name of the person or organization to whom the proposal is being submitted, the name of the proposal writer and the date.
Table of Contents	It contains content with page numbers.
List of Figures	This section includes a list of tables, graphs, figures and charts used in the proposal.
Abstract or Summary	An abstract or a summary is a brief version of the proposal.
Methodology	It summarizes the proposed methods of data collection and the procedure for investigating the situation and problem.
Introduction	This section introduces readers to the proposal. It gives the background, states the purpose and discusses the scope.
Statement of the problem	This section
Proposed plan and schedule	This section presents a schedule of activities highlighting the main course of action.
Advantages /Disadvantages	This section highlights advantages and disadvantages of your project.
Recommendations	It is the most persuasive section of a proposal. It is usually the longest section of proposal and is logically structured into small sub sections.
Conclusion	This section presents the final summary of the proposal and focuses on main points and the key benefits and advantages.
Appendix	Appendix includes secondary or extra information. Tables, flow charts, maps are generally included.

28. JOB APPLICATION

Types of Resume

(1) Chronological Resume : Chronological resume focuses/emphasizes on education and experience. It lists entries in reverse order, beginning with most recent experience and degree.

(2) Functional Resume : Functional resume focuses on professional skills developed during your employment rather than on the when, where and what of each position. It organizes your experience in terms of skills and accomplishments.

(3) Combination/Hybrid Resume : Combination resume is a combination of both the chronological and the functional format. It demonstrates your skills and experience as themes and then your employment experience follows chronologically.

(4) Electronic Resume : An electronic resume, also called a scannable resume, is a plain text (ASCII) or HTML document, often submitted with an employment application, that uses keywords to provide an employer with information regarding a job candidate's professional experience, education, and job qualifications.

Advantages :

(1) Numerous employers can access it instantly

(2) Graphics, animation or sound can be included

(3) It can be updated quickly & easily

Parts of Job Application

An application is made of two essential parts:

(1) Resume (2) Cover Letter or Application Letter.

Resume includes

(A) Heading : It includes Name, Address , phone no

(B) Job Objective : Job objective should state what you want to do.

(C) Education Qualification : List all your relevant education, training, and certifications. List degrees(s) awarded, year of graduation/completion

(D) Work Experience include the name of the employer, geographic location (city and state only), position title, dates of employment, a brief statement of duties and your major contributions

(E) Resume   also includes Achievement /Awards, Special Skills, Hobbies, References etc.

Cover Letter or Application Letter includes

- Date, Writer's address, Recipient's address, Subject,
- Saluation.
- Introduction. (It includes Mention from where you discovered the job applying, Mention specific job you are applying for)
- Conclusion is an optimist call for interview. It can be written e.g. I wish to hear from you soon Give your contact numbers

Difference between Resume and Curriculum Vitae

A resume is a one or two page summary of your skills, experience and education. While a resume is brief and concise - no more than a page or two, a Curriculum Vitae is a longer (at least two page) and more detailed synopsis. A Curriculum Vitae includes a summary of your educational and academic backgrounds as well as teaching and research experience, publications, presentations, awards, honors, affiliations and other details.

Importance of Resume

Resumes tell a lot about you to your employer. Your resume will have details which consist of form where you have been, where you are at present and where you are headed.. Your resume will self-give a confidence which tells about you to the interviewer. The main objective of a resume is winning a job, interview by highlighting the applicants fitness for a particular position.

Tips for writing Resume :

(1) Avoid writing text

(2) Use short sentences

(3) Be brief

(4) Avoid spelling and grammatical errors

(5) List your achievements/awards/skills in sequence

(6) Do not exaggerate your achievements

(7) Be reasonable in showing your achievements/skills

(8) Make resume reader oriented

SAMPLE OF JOB APPLICATION

XYZ

Anand-Vidyanagar

Anand

9th July, 2010

To,

The Manager

Sales India, Anand

Dear Sir,

      Sub : An Application for the Post of _____.

With reference to your advertisement in _____ on (date), I would like to apply for the above mentioned post.

I request you to judge my candidature and competence in the light of my enclosed resume.

I eagerly await your call for personal interview.

                Yours faithfully,

                Chintan A. Mahida

SAMPLE OF RESUME

Mr. XYZ

Anand

Personal Details : It includes Nationality, Blood Group, Weight, Height, **Status**

Position Sought : …………………………………………………..

Career Objective : ………………………………………………..

Experience   : (1) Most Recent entry comes first

                    (2) …………………………………………..

Qualification   : (1) Most Recent entry comes first

                    (2) …………………………………………..

Special   Skills   : ………………………………………………...

Interest   : ………………………………………………..

Awards   : …………………………………………………

Achievement   : …………………………………………………

References   : (1) Name of the person, address

                    (2) Name of the person, address

BIBLIOGRAPHY

1) Andersen, Richard. Powerful Writing Skills. New York:Barnes & Noble Books, 2001.
2) Angell, David, and Brent Heslop. The Elements of E-Mail Style: Communicate Effectively Via ElectronicMail. Boston: Addison-Wesley, 1994.
3) Bly, Robert. Encyclopedia of Business Letters, Fax Memos, and E-Mail. Franklin Lakes, N.J.: Career Press, Incorporated, 1999.
4) Bond, Alan. 300 Successful Business Letters.Hauppauge, N.Y.: Barron's Educational Series,Incorporated, 1998.
5) Carnegie, Dale. The Quick and Easy Way to EffectiveSpeaking. New York: Pocket Books, 1990.
6) Chang, Richard, and Kevin Kehoe. Meetings ThatWork! A Practical Guide to Shorter and MoreProductive Meetings. San Francisco, Calif.: Jossey- Bass, 1994.unningham,
7) Helen, and Brenda Greene. TheBusiness Style Handbook: An A-to-Z Guide for Writingon the Job with Tips from Communications Experts at the Fortune 500. New York: McGraw-Hill, 2002.
8) Griffin, Jack. How to Say It at Work: Putting YourselfAcross with Power Words, Phrases, Body Language and Communication Secrets. New York: Prentice Hall Press, 1998.
9) Jeary, Tony. Inspire Any Audience: Proven Secrets of thePros for Powerful Presentations. Dallas: Trophy Publishing, 1996.
10)   Lindsell-Roberts, Sheryl. Writing Business Letters For Dummies. Hoboken, N.J.: John Wiley & Sons, 1999.
11)   King, Stephen. On Writing: A Memoir of the Craft.Southern Pines, N.C.: Scribner, 2002.
12)   Martin, Paul. Wall Street Journal Guide to Business Styleand Usage. New York: The Free Press, 2002.
13)   Matejka, Ken, and Diane P. Ramos. Hook 'Em: Speakingand Writing to Catch and Keep a Business Audience.New York: AMACOM, 1996.
14)   Mosvick, Roger, and Robert Nelson. We've Got To StartMeeting Like This! A Guide to Successful MeetingManagement. Indianapolis, Ind.: JIST Works, 1997.
15)   Paolo, Frank. How To Make a Great Presentation in 2Hours. Hollywood, Fla.: Lifetime Books, 1994.132 Communication Skills Plotnik, Arthur. The Elements of Expression. Lincoln,Nebr.: iUniverse, 2000.

16)   Richardson, Bradley G. Jobsmarts for Twenty-somethings. New York: Vintage, 1995.

17)   Roman, Kenneth, and Joel Raphaelson. Writing ThatWorks: How to Communicate Effectively in Business.New York: HarperResource, 2000.

18)   Sant, Tom. Persuasive Business Proposals: Writing toWin Customers, Clients, and Contracts. New York: AMACOM, 1992.

19)   Simmons, Curt. Public Speaking Made Simple. Burlington, Mass.: Made Simple, 1996.

20)   Strunk, William. The Elements of Style, Fourth Edition. Boston: Allyn & Bacon, 1999.

21)   Walton, Donald. Are You Communicating? New York: McGraw-Hill, 1991.